Ali Hamidi's
CARP
FISHING
MASTERCLASS

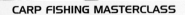

CONTENTS

FOREWORD

Ali Hamidi, in a relatively short period of time, has become one of the most recognisable faces in modern carp fishing. Through his role with Korda, and the subsequent media coverage that he and the company have enjoyed, we have all come to know and like him immensely. The fella can also write very well, as I am sure you are about to find out in Carp Fishing Masterclass.

The thing I like the most about Ali is that he understands where it's at in terms of carp fishing. Although he has actually been fishing a long time and is well versed in the history in which the sport is steeped, Ali prefers to focus on the future and, in particular, helping newcomers enjoy their fishing and, ultimately, catch more carp. This has certainly been my experience of him when he has fulfilled the numerous magazine features for my title.

Similarly to Total Carp, Ali has a desire to help others and nowhere is this better reflected than in this very book. With chapters on all aspects of carping, including watercraft, rigs, technique, fish care, stalking and a few little 'left-field' edges, there is most definitely something in here to help everybody, regardless of skill level. However, it is in the simple presentation of all of these tips and tactics that this book really excels. Easy to follow and not full of difficult idiosyncrasies which many find hard to keep abreast of, Carp Fishing Masterclass is a kind of handbook and one that I am sure thousands of you will keep, as a reference tool, for a very long time.

Enjoy this book and, more importantly, enjoy your carp fishing, which I am sure will be all the richer and more successful for you having absorbed what you are about to read. Tight lines and all that...

Marc Coulson

Marc Coulson is the editor of Total Carp, the UK's biggest-selling carp fishing magazine.

INTRODUCTION

As I sit here looking at the finished proofs of this book, I feel quite emotional about it all to be honest. From the humble beginnings of living in Iran and hiding in bomb shelters as the Iraqi's attacked my birthplace of Esfahan, its quite unbelievable to think I've become an angler with enough experience to feel brave enough to put pen to paper and finish my first book. Most Asian kids are pressured by their parents to become Doctors or Lawyers, but fair play to my amazing family and more importantly Soheila and Seraj (mum & dad) who have backed me in whatever I've done. They're proud that I've pursued my passion and turned it into a career, and I'll always be grateful to the people that helped open doors for me at the beginning and during my carp fishing journey.

Special thanks firstly to Tim Paisley, Simon Crow and Julian Cundiff for giving me a chance to have my first articles printed in Carpworld during 2002. Steve Morgan and Kev Knight at Mainline Baits for being such a huge support for so many years and showing so much faith in me when I was just a teenager. Also to my very good friend Chris Cockerell at Sky TV who has helped Korda to bring Thinking Tackle and numerous other TV projects to your screens. To Danny Fairbrass and Damian Clarke, for seeing a glimmer of talent and employing me at Korda. I left a successful marketing career and took a punt in joining Korda, but it has been the best decision I've ever made. Not a day goes by that you don't look forward to going to work. Marc Coulson and DHP for helping collate the hundreds of images in this book, without their continued support and assistance this book wouldn't have been possible. AND finally the many friends and anglers I have met through my beloved passion, its all of our experiences together that has given me the ammunition to write a technical book like this, and the old adage of "you can learn something from everyone" has never rung so true.

Onto the book itself, its main focus is to help anglers of all abilities to put fish on the bank. In everything I do, I always try my best and endeavour to become the best even if I fall short. However this attitude has meant I have tried to hone my angling skills in a manner of carp fishing disciplines, which I hope this book reflects. Whether you're in your first year of carp fishing or an experienced pro, I hope there are tips that will help all of you increase your catch rate. With everything from watercraft to bait rolling covered, I hope you too can produce a carp fishing masterclass in your fishing. If this book helps all of you to put an extra carp on the bank or even a PB, then you can be sure I'll be proud that the hard work has paid off. Read it, digest it, follow the tips, fish with confidence and let the good times roll!

Happy fishing and good health,

Ali Hamidi

WATERCRAFT

In today's fishing climate we are spoilt for choice with the array of fishing tackle that is available to us. We have top quality bait, reels, rods and tackle at our disposal. All of these have made carp fishing more accessible to the masses, and have given an opportunity to newcomers to get amongst the action much quicker. However one single thing is infinitely more important than any bait or item of tackle, it's the single most important thing in your carp fishing armoury and the only thing you can't buy in a bag, we could call it the X-factor, but its far simpler, it's WATERCRAFT.

It's no use having the best tackle in the world and then choosing a swim or area of a lake with no fish present. You need to learn to assess the lake based on weather conditions, features and other general topography. It's an element of your angling that develops with experience. The more you catch the more you learn. I am still stunned when I watch people turn up at a lake, and then proceed to park themselves in the nearest swim without giving it a second thought. They then sit there and watch fish leap from the water like 'flipper' in another part of the lake and take no notice of the fact that they are fishing nowhere near the main group of fish. Of course laziness plays a part in peoples fishing. However I don't know about you, but I don't go fishing to sit there and get cold do you?

This is why I am making this the first key subject in this book, because it's the most important! Without honing your watercraft skills and sensory perception, you will always remain an average angler. Get your fish locating skills sorted and you're on the super highway to success. Good location coupled with the simple rig that I'm covering in this chapter will be enough to get any budding angler off to a contented start.

Like anything, it's easy for accomplished anglers to sit there and tell you it's easy, but fish location isn't an exact science. Sometimes it can be extremely difficult to second guess where the fish might be, especially when it's freezing cold and lifeless in mid-January, but this is where you draw on past experiences to help push you in the right direction. Key components play a part in shaping your chain of thought and this is what I'm going to cover, which I hope will help you finish the location jigsaw in style.

WIND

Ask any avid carp-angler, what's your favourite carp fishing conditions, I'm sure you'll get a familiar reply along these lines; "a medium strength south-westerly wind in your face, with a low pressure cloud cover, drizzle and light showers". You know you're going to catch in these conditions. It's generally a low pressure band of weather from the SW and 8/9 months of the year through spring, summer and autumn, when the big southerlies blow, and you get in the teeth of them, the fishing can be hot. However this is a perfect scenario. In other less predictable conditions, you need to adjust your approach.

For example, winds from the east are cooler and can be a real turn-off for fish, an old saying is "wind from the east, the fish bite least"! This is ironically very true. When an easterly is blowing, I try to fish away from the wind. Try to look for areas at the back of the wind line and away from the main 'bite' of the cold wind. Other hot spots in these conditions are areas of cover and backs of islands which are in the 'lee' of the wind.

I could write thousands of words on wind direction, but generally in cooler weather, stay off the back of cold winds, but fish in the face of milder winds from the south or south west. The low pressure pushes fish down to feed hard, whilst high pressure cold days, can lift fish off the bottom and make them very sporadic feeders. Study wind direction, check the weather on the net before you go on sites such as www.metcheck.com or www.bbc.co.uk/weather.

BUBBLERS

One of the first things I learnt to look for as a budding carp angler was bubbles. It was like my hallowed sign. Ever since then I have always kept my eyes glued on the surface for signs of feeding fish through the medium of bubbles! When the surface is calm it is very simple to spot bubbling carp. However you need to distinguish between what's feeding fish, and what's natural gases being released from the lakebed. Natural gases tend to get released in a consistent pattern one after another, almost like bubbles rising from the bottom of a glass of coke.

However 'carpy' bubbles tend to be more sporadic and can rise in quite a big area, or often in a trail. Casting into bubblers can often result in opportune captures. Additionally, when you are feeding freebies into certain areas, these are a tell-tale sign, as to whether fish are on your bait, or not. Generally bubbles are more apparent when fish feed on a soft bottom, as a result they are far easier to spot on this. Keep your eyes peeled on slow days for signs of bubblers, even if its bream or tench feeding, the carp won't be far away.

COLOURED WATER

Sometimes the most subtle signs are the best ones. It still surprises me when people ignore coloured water. Carp can be aggressive feeders even in the coldest of weather, as a result when they feed it is inevitable that the area where they choose to feed is more coloured than normal. On clear waters this can be far more obvious than on mud or clay coloured lakes. However if you look closely enough it is still possible to pick out the contrast in water colour. Therefore if there are no visible fish signs then keep your eye out for areas of coloured water, especially if you have limited fishing time like myself. Sometimes casting into a 'cloudy' bit of water can result in a quick bite.

WATER OUTFLOW

If fishing is slow, then explore oxygenated water inflows. If a water you're fishing has aerators or inflow pipes, then keep an eye on these when it's high pressure and hot, then get a rod near these areas when they are switched on, fish often swarm around them when they are turned on. Action can be instant.

REEDS

Similarly to snags, fish love reeds! I will never forget the first time I sat with my eyes glued to a set of reeds, only to see one of the stems shake completely out of tune with the wind. This was in fact a 'reed warbler', the term used to describe what happens when a fish swims through reeds and disturbs the stems. Like snags, reeds hold fish all year round. Carp like to use them as sanctuary and to also clean themselves after a semi dormant winter, where they will have picked up leeches and parasites on their body. Keep your eyes peeled on reedbeds to look for 'warblers'. In the summer months, reeds will be a real hot spot due to the popularity of them during spawning and the warm weather.

SNAGS

Ever since I started carp fishing, I don't think I've ever been to a lake with snags that the carp do not regularly visit. If ever there was a feature that screams carp, its snags! Overhangs, dense foliage, roots and even old shopping trolleys slumped in the water will hold fish. Carp love features and cover. It's their safe haven away from angler's lines, as a result you will almost definitely find fish in snags. They might not be easy to get feeding near snags, but if you want to guarantee you're near a carp or two, then snags are never a bad bet. In cold conditions, fish like to take sanctuary in snags because the water stays a more constant temperature as it isn't exposed to the elements as much. If a lake is featureless, but has an area of snags somewhere, then fish will almost certainly use this as a regular hiding 'haunt'. It can be frustrating from a fishing perspective, but as a kid I spent hundreds of hours sat up trees in snags watching fish, happy memories and a great education to watch fish enjoying their environment.

AWAY FROM ANGLING PRESSURE

With the rise of day ticket fisheries and anglers alike, lakes are becoming more and more pressured with the fish seeing every trick in the book. Fish are becoming more accustomed to recognising dangerous areas to feed based on the visibility of mainlines and also swimming and brushing up against lines. It's no coincidence that whenever I visit pressured lakes, the fish are continually doing 'carp acrobatics' in the one swim or area where there are no lines. It's perfectly natural that fish will move away from continued baiting and casting out. As a result whenever I visit such lakes I try to concentrate my approach in parts of the lake that are not being fished. If there are 5 anglers in a line, then don't be the 6th. Go and look for fish where there is less angling pressure, fish will almost certainly be there and feeding more comfortably.

BIRD LIFE

This has proven to be one of my winter location saviours. On occasions when I haven't seen a lake or am unaware of past captures in the coldest of weather, I'm always interested to see where the biggest flock of birds are holding up. I have lost count of the amount of times I have spotted rare sightings of fish right in the middle of a flock of coots or tutfties! I always say the birds are there for a reason.

WATER DEPTH

Water depth is a critical factor in pinpointing carp all year round. If it's sweltering hot and the lake you fish has a shallow area then you can bet your bottom dollar that the fish will be frequenting this area regularly. Another thing to bear in mind, even in the depths of winter is that fish will still visit shallow water. On sunny days, shallow areas are going to warm up much quicker, as a result fish often investigate these areas in rare feeding spells, so always keep your eyes peeled on these spots.

Deep water is slightly less predictable. In low pressure bands of weather the fish often push to the bottom and will feed with gusto. However in high air pressure conditions the water depth can be far more critical in deciding the shape of your session. Fish can often be roaming a long way off the bottom, in mid-water to quarter depth. As a result you need to be aware of this and not concentrate all of your approach on the bottom. I'm a huge believer in Zig rig fishing, which is basically a suspended floating bait, that can be presented off the bottom straight off your lead. This is a devastating tactic . So be aware that when the lake is slow all round with no one catching, it means fish could be off the bottom, therefore you need to present a bait to them there.

A RIG TO GET STARTED

The following rig is very basic, and one that I still use today. It may be simple to tie, but will catch you plenty of fish in the right circumstances. To tie this rig you will need the following components, IQ Soft 10lb, Size 12 Korda Wide Gape hooks, a Ring swivel Safezone leader, Korda lead clip, tail rubber and a small 2oz Distance lead.

01

The components that you will need to tie the following rig.

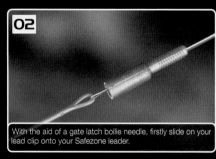

02

With the aid of a gate latch boilie needle, firstly slide on your lead clip onto your Safezone leader.

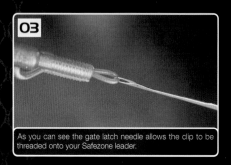

03

As you can see the gate latch needle allows the clip to be threaded onto your Safezone leader.

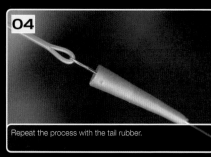

04

Repeat the process with the tail rubber.

05

At the end of your ring swivel Safezone leader will be a Korda size 8 ring swivel already attached.

06

Now pull the leader so the swivel 'clicks' into the lead clip. If it doesn't click you haven't pulled hard enough.

07

Now slide the swivel of your lead onto the arm of the lead clip.

08

Salivate the lead clip and then slide the tail rubber over the lead clip.

09

Push the tail rubber about half way over the body of the clip. Not the whole way as this could stop the lead from discharging if it gets snagged.

10

Now tie your mainline to the other end of the Safezone leader with the aid of a Palomar knot. Then you're finished, now for the hooklink.

11

Firstly start by making a simple overhand loop at the end of your Korda IQ soft hooklink.

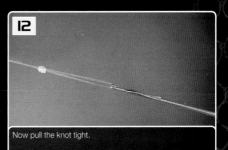

12

Now pull the knot tight.

13

These Mainline dumbbells are great hookbaits when fishing for pressured carp that have been caught one too many times on round boilies. The shape change can make all the difference, coupled with the amazing aroma.

14

Now thread your mainline Pulse dumbbell on your gate latch needle.

15

Thread onto the hair and finish with a boilie stop.

16

Now take a hook out the packet and ensure you check the sharpness against your skin to make sure you have a 'super sharp' one.

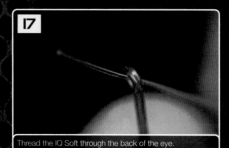

17

Thread the IQ Soft through the back of the eye.

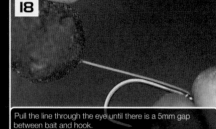

18

Pull the line through the eye until there is a 5mm gap between bait and hook.

19

Now commence tying the knotless knot. Whip away from the seam in the hook.

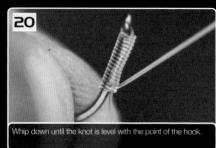

20

Whip down until the knot is level with the point of the hook.

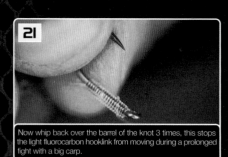

21

Now whip back over the barrel of the knot 3 times, this stops the light fluorocarbon hooklink from moving during a prolonged fight with a big carp.

22

Now pass the tag of the line through the back of the eye.

Slowly pull the knot under tension with the aid of a Korda Pulla tool. This fastens and secures the knot perfectly.

Now tie the other end to the ring swivel on your lead system with the aid of a 5 turn grinner knot. Your rig is now complete.

SUMMARY

This is the most vital element of carp fishing. The old adage of 5 minutes in the right swim is better than 24 hours in the wrong swim is so true. It's a subject that I could write a whole book on, and still not do it justice. You will hone your skills the more you visit venues and look for fish. It really is the single element that separates the average from the exceptional.

As a result all the best bait, rigs and mod cons, can never compete with an angler that has perfected his watercraft. If you track down the fish and put yourself in a swim with feeding fish, then any rig will fool any carp! Good luck.

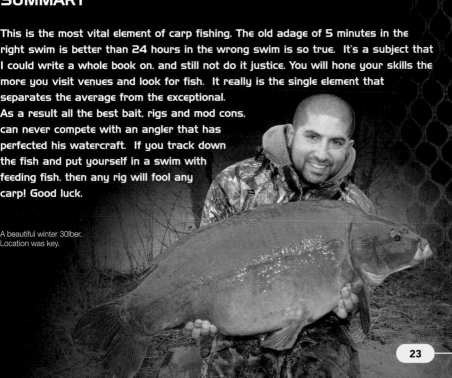

A beautiful winter 30lber. Location was key.

FEATURE FINDING

Having eyes underwater would give every angler on this planet a major advantage when targeting their quarry. Unfortunately none of us have that luxury and we are as blind as Stevie Wonder when it comes to guessing what's going on in the great 'abyss' of some venues.

Learning to read the make-up of the terrain that you are fishing over is one of the most vital assets that any angler can have in their armoury. Of course on their day, any angler will catch by chucking and chancing it, but that person will never catch as many as the guy who has carefully located an underwater feature, which will almost certainly be a natural feeding area. To many beginners this will seem like rocket science. However I can assure you that locating features on the lake bed is a simple skill to master and one that any angler who is willing to add it into their fishing routine will benefit from instantly.

WHAT DO YOU NEED TO LOOK FOR?

Choosing the type of lake bed to present your bait and feed over comes with experience and differs from venue to venue. There are no hard and fast rules, and you will develop your own favourite spots over time. However I'm sure that some of you would like a guideline and that's what I'm going to explain now.

Finding a contrasting lakebed is important. For example, if the lake that you are fishing is predominantly silty, then look for firmer parts of lakebed, maybe shallower areas of silt or even gravel, and wherever possible, try to fish near the seam of these areas, i.e. where the softer silt meets the firmer sand or gravel. Fish will use these transitional areas as definite feeding spots. If you're fishing gravel pits or clay based lakes then, then look for areas with softer lake beds. Food *lardae* will often hold up in these areas and fish will visit these spots and feed because they differ to the majority of the lakebed.

A lot of newcomers to the sport are scared of weed, don't be. If a lake you are fishing has weedy areas then make sure you are fishing as close to it as humanly possible because weed carries so much natural food that the carp can't help but visit these area. Most anglers are scared of fishing in weed because they are worried about their presentation. However a simple PVA bag set-up and a long hooklink will help you combat weed. Just make sure if you find some, you fish in it or near it.

These are some basic principles that I learnt at a young age and they have put me in good stead ever since. Throughout the picture sequences I will talk to you about what the differing lakebeds feel like when transmitted through rod and line and some instrumental tackle requirements.

FINDING GRAVEL

Gravel is probably the most easily recognised feature when using a marker float. With the aid of braided mainline, you will feel that very recognisable tap tap tap through the rod tip. When you retrieve the marker system along the lakebed, if the rod is bending very little and transmitting a very consistent vibrating sensation then you know you're on gravel. The more pronounced the 'taps', the larger the rocks that you're fishing over. Lumpy gravel is not always the best area to present a bait, as it can make presentations inconsistent, however small pea type gravel has always been a superb place to present a bait.

FINDING SILT

Assessing the depth of the silt you are fishing in can be quite tricky, however if you follow a few simple rules then you won't go far wrong. When you cast into silt, immediately the lead will feel plugged. The tip will bend round and then you will slowly feel the lead come back. The retrieve should be smooth and consistent, however the way to gauge the depth is by looking at the rod tip. The deeper the silt the more bent your tip will be. I don't particularly like fishing in very deep silt as this can be rancid and not great to present a bait in, this is also affectionately known as 'chod'. However shallower silt surrounded by harder lake beds can be a great place to position a hookbait

FINDING WEED

Casting into weed can instantly feel like you have cast into deep silt. However as soon as you begin to retrieve the marker system, you will feel a jerking sensation as the lead tears through weed into a small clearing and then straight back into weed. Once again, the heavier the weed, the harder it will be to retrieve the lead. Heavy weed can be a nightmare to fish in, but with some careful feature finding you will very quickly learn to distinguish between what is fishable and what isn't. A nice simple rule that I like to use, is if the marker float pops up, the area is fish-able, however if the float struggles to rise then it's probably not a good idea to cast there. If you can find gravel clearings near weed-beds then you're onto a winner. Obviously if you're using Marker Stems, the float is more likely to pop to the surface. So if you want to distinguish just how savage the weed is, then take the stem off and have the marker lead running on your mainline. This will mean that the float will only rise comfortably if the marker lead is not too hindered.

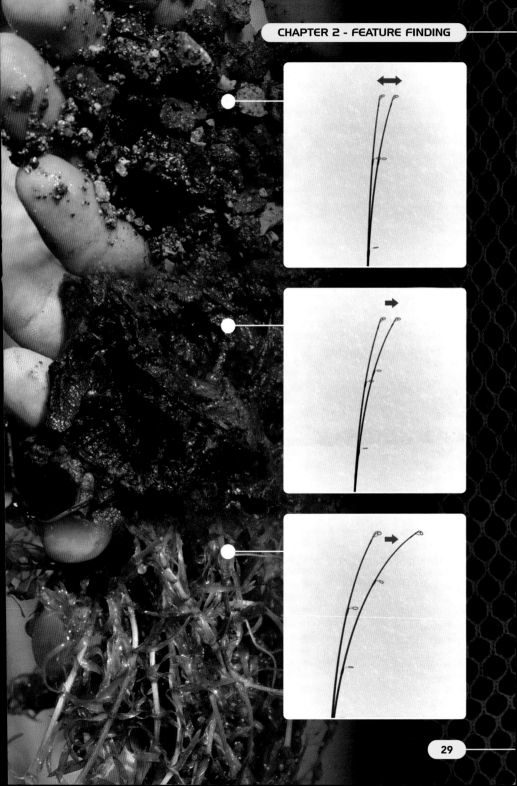

MARKER FLOAT SYSTEM

For all carp anglers, the marker float is a phenomenal tool. It really is an essential approach and you must all learn to use it effectively. It can be a little confusing to set-up, but the following sequence shows off a system that I like to use, and if you follow the step-by-step you will realise just how easy it is to do. So get your marker rod sorted and get PLUMBING.

01
The new Korda marker float kit has everything you need to set-up a complete marker float system.

02
The Drop Zone marker float has an extremely visible flight that can be seen in difficult light conditions and at very long ranges.

03
A swivel is built into the foot of the float.

04
The Drop Zone marker float is both aerodynamic and extremely buoyant, two of the most critical elements when choosing a marker float.

05
These beads help to make everything streamlined and tangle-proof, once again they come inside the excellent marker kit pack.

06
The Marker Stem is a critical addition to this pack, because it makes feature finding on weedy lakes an absolute dream. The buoyant cylinder of foam helps to lift the stem and alas the float above detritus on the bottom.

07

At the foot of the stem is a 'Stik Klip', which gives you a very simple quick change facility for the lead.

08

The new 'PROBE' lead has been specifically designed for feature finding.

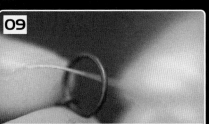

09

To set-up the marker float, firstly thread the braid through the large ring on the ring swivel of the marker stem.

10

Now thread on the large rubber bead that comes inside your marker float kit.

11

Now thread on the buffer bead that will fit snugly on the swivel at the foot of your marker float.

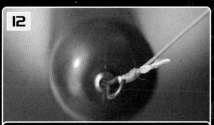

12

Next its time to tie your braid to the swivel on the float with the aid of a 5 turn grinner knot.

13

Now its time to clip the 'Probe' lead onto your stik klip on the marker stem.

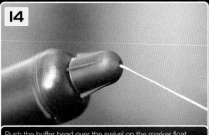

14

Push the buffer bead over the swivel on the marker float.

When feature finding, braided mainline is an absolute must. Braids like Berkeley Whiplash are extremely low in diameter which means you can cast a very long way, however more importantly, braid has zero stretch, which means it is the most accurate transmitter of sensations from lakebed to rod tip. You will feel features much quicker and far more accurately. So don't have a marker float reel, without braided mainline.

In my opinion, the stiffer the rod, the better, when it comes to feature finding. A soft rod just bends far too easily and doesn't magnify the sensations that are delivered to the rod tip with the aid of a marker system and braided mainline. Also because a marker float system is quite bulky, you need to be able to cast it long distances as your fishing develops and you move onto larger expanses of water. With a soft rod this would be impossible. As a result I use a Shimano Tribal spod rod or Beastmaster spod rod for my marker float work. It's worth spending a few extra quid on a marker rod, because in most instances, it's more important than your fishing rods.

Because Whiplash is so low in diameter, it can be prone to tangles when used straight through to the marker float. As a result I like to use 2 rod lengths of Arma-Kord in 30 or 50lb. The slightly higher diameter helps to eliminate tangles and withstand the force of extreme long distance casting.

CONCLUSION

Well that's a look at feature finding. It really is a vital tool in any angler's armoury and a skill that I hope you can all master because it's an art that will turn an average angler into a great one. Learning to read the lakebed will truly put many extra fish on the bank for you. Invest in the kit that I have covered, follow the basic rules that I have outlined and very soon you will be catching fish off spots that you have expertly found, rather than chucking and chancing it and leaving your results in the lap of the gods.

A Chilham Mill beauty caught off a clear spot in weed on a short overnighter.

HITTING THE SPOT

Hopefully after reading the last chapter on feature finding, most of you have had a chance to acquaint yourselves with the art of using a marker float and are beginning to understand the terrain of the lakebed that you are fishing. This alone will put a lot of extra fish on the bank for you. Finding natural feeding areas is half the battle when targeting specimen sized fish of any species.

In this chapter we're taking the accuracy element to a new level and are looking closely at how by fishing tightly you can turn a mediocre session into a 'red letter day'. By baiting and fishing accurately you will ensure that you keep fish feeding in a concentrated area, which in turn will intensify their feeding behaviour and make them a lot more catchable.

I see so many anglers baiting freely and casting freely without ever clipping up to the hotspot that they found with the aid of a marker float. Of course they will catch odd fish, but the best anglers have all perfected the tactic of clipping up, marking lines and fishing with pin point accuracy on every cast. Not only does it mean you can fish more accurately in the day, it also means you can cast to the same difficult to reach spots in the hours of darkness. This has to be one of the biggest problem areas for budding new specimen anglers, however by following some very simple methods, anyone can fish this effectively in no time at all. The old angling adage of effort equals reward, most certainly rings true here, and if you're willing to put these basic accuracy tips into practice I promise that your catch rate will double overnight, if not treble!

CLIPPING UP

The scenario is simple, you have spent 20mins or so, plumbing and feature finding around your swim. You have now found a small gravel area behind a bank of weed that is perfect for a few spod-full's of particle and two baited rigs, but how on earth do you ensure that everything lands perfectly on the spot and is covered accurately with a liberal amount of bait? The picture sequences will now take you through a simple yet highly effective way of getting everything 'cock-on'!

Firstly line up your marker float (which should be an area that you want your hookbait cast to) with a horizon marker such as a tall tree. This gives you a target to cast at once you are clipped up, these are also pivotal when re-casting in the dark. It's your sight marker and also a great reference point for future fishing sessions, especially if you're successful.

02

Now look down at your feet and ensure you memorise your standing point in the swim. This should remain your casting point at all times. If you are further back or further forward and are casting to snags or reeds, you are likely to lose a lot of tackle if you don't position your feet in the same spot. It might sound like a minor detail, but boy does it make a difference.

OI

03

Now carefully pull the float under by levering the rod skyward, once the float hit's the bottom, you will suddenly feel the rod bend more aggressively as the float jams against the lead on the bottom.

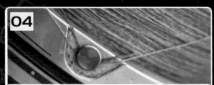

04

Now carefully put your braided mainline under the line clip a couple of times to secure your casting distance, but please ensure you do this with the rod tip in the air. The reason is that when you re-cast, as the line hits the clip, the rod tip absorbs the force and lays the lead on the water rather than crashing it in. This is very important.

05

Time to wind in.

06

Find yourself a straight area of bank behind where you're fishing and lay your marker rod down. Once you have done this, push in a tent peg directly parallel to the reel seat on the rod, this will be your first distance marker, to signify your casting point.

07

Now open the bail arm on the reel, pick up your marker float and lead and walk away into the distance until you hit the line clip which means you have walked the distance that you are clipped up to on your marker float set-up.

08

Carefully place the float and lead down and push another tent peg into the ground, this now marks the exact distance that you where casting to with the marker float, now its time to mark up your fishing rods. These pegs now act as your distance markers, if you want to use them for the duration of the session then I suggest you keep them out of harms way so no dog walkers or other anglers trip over them!

09

Firstly place your fishing rod by the first distance peg that you set by the reel seat. This signifies your starting point whenever you go to re-mark your lines.

10

Now pick up your rig and make your way towards the second tent peg which marks your distance that you want your rig to fall.

11

Once you have reached the 2nd peg, whip your rig around the peg to secure it in place.

12

Next return to the other marker where your reel is stationed and slowly tighten up the line until you feel tension, once you have done this, place your mainline under the reels line clip. I think the Shimano reel line clips are superb, but I always put my line round the clip twice just to cushion the blow of a hard cast.

13

To ensure that you reach the same spot every time without having to walk your lines out again, tie a stop knot on your mainline. This is very simple. Firstly cut off 4-5 inches of no.4 pole elastic. Hold parallel against your line about 1ft from your reel.

14

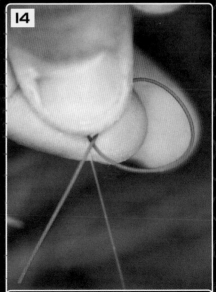

Make a loop by crossing each end and once again hold the base of the loop parallel to the mainline.

15

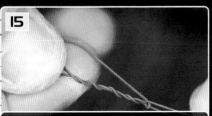

With one tag end, wrap the elastic around the line and through the loop, almost like a grinner, but remembering to sandwich the mainline in-between. Repeat this process four times.

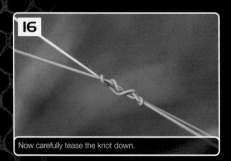

16

Now carefully tease the knot down.

17

Here is the knot pulled down nice and tight. Ensure that it doesn't move up and down the line as this will deem the stop knot ineffective because it is likely to slip during a prolonged fight with a big carp. This would then mess up your distances when you come to clipping up again.

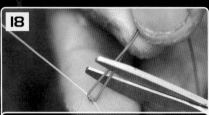

18

Cut off the tag ends leaving about 5mm at each end. This helps it fly through the rings better and also gives you a sound signal at night when you want to clip up again.

19

The finished knot looks like so. As a result, if you ever want the rig back on the same spot, go into a vacant swim next door if possible or cast into un-fished water (not someone else's swim), cast your rig, wind it back until the stop knot is 1ft from the reel and then place under the line clip again. You will now be able to cast 'slap bang' on the same spot again.

20

To ensure your spod mix and freebies land on exactly the same spot, place your spod and reel 1ft ahead of your fishing rod and reel. The reason for one foot in this situation is quite simple. After watching a lot of underwater footage and talking to many friends on the subject we have concluded that if you're fishing in 3ft of water, the lead is likely to swing back 1ft into you on a tight line. As a result, on this session I'm fishing in 3ft of water so I will be clipping my spod up, one foot short of my baited rig. This shall ensure that the freebies land directly on top of my rig. You can follow this rule of thumb for deeper water as well, for example, if you're fishing in 6ft of water I will clip my spod 2ft short of the rig. The 3:1 rule is an approximate and in no way definitive, because lead size, wind and a whole host of other variables play a part, however it's a good starting point and one that has not let me down.

21

Now walk the spod up to the 2nd peg and hook it on. Return to the spod reel, increase the tension and place under the line clip. Your spod rod is now clipped up expertly at the same distance as your rig, perfect.

DRILLING IN!

The art of edging your way up to features. What I have noticed during my many years of carp fishing is that fish don't spook too much when they're under the cover of snags or reeds. Unlike fishing in open water where carp are prone to bolting away at the sound of a lead, fish under sanctuary are not so susceptible to being spooked. So take your time and ensure you get that rig right in the carp's home and get ready for action.

01

Firstly have a cast at a feature that interests you, in this instance it's a reed bed that I really fancy some action off. However I deliberately cast short of the spot. I estimate that I have landed 2ft short of where I want my rig to land.

02

With the rod pointing at the sky, I pay off 2ft of line from the reel.

03

Now place the line under the clip. Have another exploratory cast, if you're still short of where you want to be, then pay off a bit more line so that you edge yourself closer to the spot. However remember two key points, ensure that your feet are positioned in the same spot when you cast and also that similarly to when you clipped up, as your lead is about to land, ensure the rod tip is pointing skyward so that everything is equal to when you clipped up.

04

If you do it right, your next cast will be as good as this, tight, and right in the carps lair!

It might seem a simple element of fishing, but I can't stress enough how important this is. It truly is the monumental difference between catching only one or 20 on your next trip! On today's very short session I followed my own advice and worked my rig into a little hole in the reeds and fooled a beautiful mid double in under half an hour. Testimony indeed, that if we fish accurately and bait accurately, we'll all catch a lot more specimens in the future.

BAITING TOOLS

For the newcomer it must be very confusing to see the array of different baiting tools and to truly understand what purpose each serves under different circumstances. Over the next few pages I'll take you through a simple 'how to' guide of the different tools and their uses. By adding this into your armoury you'll be able to feed bait accurately at different ranges.

THE CATAPULT

This is probably the longest serving tool in the history of angling. I have owned a catapult for baiting up ever since I first started angling and its still my favourite. Unfortunately the angling market doesn't produce reliable ones yet but I'm sure some of the better companies will produce something soon that will last the test of time. So what's special about a catapult? For short-range work there is nothing better. However if you want to feed accurately then the bait you use must be the same size inside the catapult. If you use different sizes and weights of bait then you will have the smaller stuff falling short and the bigger baits landing long which isn't ideal. As a result if you want to use different sized baits like mixed pellets or boilies, then separate them first and introduce them separately but onto the same spot. This way you will get mixed size baits introduced accurately which will induce a much better feeding response as the fish will be unable to distinguish between the hookbait and the freebies.

The more sizes of bait that you have out there the harder it will be for them to suss you out. For boilie fishing at short-medium range (5yards to 50yards), you can't beat a catapult. One trick that I use to vary the spray of bait is to angle the catapult skyward. Think of yourself stood up and the surface of the lake as the axis of a right angle. The higher you aim the tighter the bait will land in your target area, the lower you aim the greater the spread of bait. There is no right or wrong answer with regards to what is a better method, but when using larger baits such as boilies, I like to spread my bait. This gets fish moving and looking for food, which then gives them less chance to investigate the baited rig. With smaller particles, the catapult does limit you to not a lot more than 10yards or so. It gives a pool table size spread which isn't great when trying to set small traps in the margins, but on heavily stocked venues it's a good way to introduce bait little and often.

THE THROWING STICK

This is quite simply an awesome boilie baiting tool. Its main purpose was to introduce single baits beyond the range of a catapults capability. It does this comfortably but needs a bit of practice. The pictures should give you an indication of the action that is required to get baits out a long way, but practice truly makes perfect in this case. With a big cross wind, its hard to be accurate with a throwing stick, however as I mentioned previously, I like a big spread of boilies as this gets the fish looking and makes them a lot easier to catch when they are moving at speed. It's also deadly at short range. When I'm using just boilies in my fishing, and I'm looking to introduce large quantities quickly, I will often put 4-5 baits in the stick at the same time.

The technique is slightly different as you need to aim high, but it helps you get a nice spread of bait quickly. For short or longer night sessions I really like the throwing stick. As I can trickle bait in quickly at different ranges and hopefully entice interest from the fish. Obviously its difficult to be deadly accurate all the time with such an instrument, however with practice you'll soon have baits hurtling out a long way. One thing worth remembering is that when trying to put baits out over 50yards or so, a slightly harder boilie is required as the throwing stick spins the baits out and has a tendency to split the bait before it reaches the distance required. Most shelf life baits are fine as they are the firmer protein or birdfood boilies.

However steer clear of soft fishmeal baits as these will split almost every time. If you want to use these baits then you will need to air-dry your baits to toughen them up. The throwing stick is a method that I use regularly and I truly believe it helps my fishing on shorter sessions due to its quickness and ease of use when introducing boilies beyond catapult range.

THE SPOD

The spod is probably the most specialist baiting tool on the market and something that very few anglers apart from carp anglers use. I find this hard to understand because in the right hands it is a devastating tactic and a great way to build multiple captures. I have already shown you how to clip up the spod accurately, so that the bait lands directly on your baited rig. However you're probably wondering why you would use a spod over other baiting tools? The answer is simple. Firstly it is the most effective way of getting small particle baits out an extremely long way. I'm not a huge caster in carping terms but with the Skyraider spod by Korda, I can fish at ranges up to a 130yards with ease. Expert long distance caster Mark Hutchinson can put the same spod over 200 yards! That's obscene, but it just goes to show why it has such a significant place in carp fishing. How else would you introduce small particles to an island margin at 100 yards? Boats and bait boats are the only real alternatives.

Particles and non aero-dynamic baits are the ideal choice in spods as there isn't anything else to really get them any distance. However the spod can be used at close range as well because its possible to underarm the spod next to marginal bushes and foliage whilst introducing a very accurate tight bed of bait. I rate the spod so highly that I very rarely go fishing without it.

The new Mini-Skyliner is even more versatile, because it is both small and superbly aero-dynamic this means you do not need specialist spodding kit to use it. If you want to learn to spod then I can' t think of anything better than the Korda mini-skyliner to get you started. By following my tips in the previous chapter regarding clipping up, you will be able to land the spod accurately and quietly on the surface of the lake. This will add another dimension to your fishing. My friends and I rate the spod so highly that on many well stocked venues, using one will literally turn 1 bite into 20. That's how big an impact it will have on your fishing. Learn to use it properly and you won't go far wrong. I have included a simple spod mix that I rate very highly which will get you off to a flying start.

As I emphasised before, the larger spods when being used at long ranges of 70 yards plus, generally need specialist spod rods and long distance reels. Stiff rods can absorb the 6-8oz weight of the spod as it compresses the carbon in the rod, whilst a normal carp rod will struggle to deal with the continued abuse and will not be able to deliver a spod accurately or very far. If you want to get started and learn to spod then use the mini-skyliner, attach it to your normal carp rods and you won't go far wrong. Don't fear the spod, EMBRACE IT!

SPOD MIX

01

The items you need for the spod mix.

02

Firstly add half a tub of Bait-techs awesome chilli-hemp, I'd be lost without this stuff.

03

Next introduce half a tub of bait-techs mixed particle.

04

Add a whole tin of corn.

05

Time to add some Mainline Fussion boilies.

06

Now chop up some different size Mainline Fusion boilies and add these into the mix.

07

The consistency should look like so, a nice variation in size and colour.

08

Now add half a bag of Mojo groundbait. This not only gives the bait a beautiful meaty scent and an irresistible cloud to the mix, it also helps bind the mix.

09

You want the mix to be tacky but not stiff so it binds, just sticky enough to hold in the spod.

I hope this chapter has given you a few ideas and has inspired you to try the spod and the throwing stick. They really will make a difference to your fishing as they will separate you from the pack, and allow you to try different baits at different ranges which I'm in no doubt will up your catch rate considerably.

ESSENTIAL KIT

In this chapter I'm going to cover the essential kit that you need to get you started in style. As a beginner, the choice today is greater than it's ever been. There are more rods, reels and luggage than ever before, at various quality and price points. Hopefully by reading this I can point you one step closer to making the right decisions when you come to handing over your hard earned cash. I remember when I first started carp fishing, it was difficult to understand just what you need and when you need it. As a result, I have highlighted over the next few pages instrumental elements in my tackle armoury, which help my fishing and ultimately results.

The range of rods available these days is frightening. There are so many to choose from! My advice may sound obvious, but please try to maximise your budget. I see so many people go out there and waste £30-£40 on a cheap rod from an unknown brand only for it to depreciate rapidly meaning your back in the market in no time at all. Firstly buy from a reputable brand such as Shimano. Companies like them are big and established for a reason. They have developed quality products consistently for decades. Similarly to buying a car or a TV, stick to solid brands that will offer you after sales and long-term guarantee's. There are too many 'flash in pan' brands in angling, stick to the established ones. With regards to rod choice, go for something with a fish playing action (medium taper/through-action), with a 12ft 2.75lb TC. This will be a good rod to start with, as it will be powerful enough if you need to cast PVA bags 50-60yards, but also good for close range fishing. The through-action should make battles with carp exciting, yet still allowing you to get control of the fight

when necessary. Unless you're going to progress to long range fishing quickly, this sort of rod will be ideal for a good few years, especially if you buy from the bigger brands I have recommended.

You're going to need a bite alarm. The ones pictured here are my Delkim TXI's, which are basically the best alarm on the market with a retail price of around £100. However Delkim also have a more cost effective option called the Delkim EV, which still has tone, sensitivity and volume adjustment. These are based on a vibration system, which is far more effective for bite registration than a standard roller buzzer. There are lots of bite alarm options on the market, but once again, stick to quality.

Similarly to rods, please avoid some of the cheap reels that are finding there way into our market. What's better, buying one reel for £60 or buying a £30 reel 3 times? I have never used anything but a Shimano reel and they have reels to suit every budget. They are the masters of gearing and lead the pack on every front when it comes to reels. The Shimano 'Baitrunner' is probably the most famous reel brand on the market and is accessible at a range of budgets. If you're looking for a good mid range budget reel, then that would be ideal. The ones pictured here are slightly larger in size and are called the Ultegra XTB, these I use for almost all my fishing up to 90 yards. They are slightly more expensive which might suit some people. However any reel from the Shimano range will stand the test of time. The Baitrunner size reel will cover your fishing needs until you step up to extreme range, and it will also compliment the rods, which I've covered.

You will be needing a landing net of approx 42" in width which will keep you covered for any likely leviathans that you're going to do battle with. Don't risk harming a beautiful carp in a small pan net that is likely to bend and  harm double figure carp. There are lots on the market at various budgets, however try to get a reasonably lightweight one, and also invest in a net float, this helps greatly when netting fish on your own, as your net won't sink in the margins as you do battle with a big carp!

Once you have the fish safely in the confines of your net, you need to ensure you have an ample sized carp mat to rest the fish on. This is a compulsory requirement on most fisheries these days. Once again there are lots available, and it's a small price to pay, when you consider you're maintaining the health and welfare of our beloved quarry!

Being comfortable when you're fishing helps, especially on the ol' back! For most of you beginning carp fishing, you'll be doing a lot of day sessions. For the past few years I have used bedchairs and chairs from Trakker, and I can honestly say I've had no problems. A small adjustable chair like the one pictured here is ideal, its also lightweight and easily transportable. Ideal for day sessions. If you want to progress to night fishing then check out their excellent range of bedchairs and all season sleeping bags.

I've had the same FOX tackle box for years now. It's the best one that's currently available, with room for additional compartments that can be purchased separately. Most of my end tackle bits are stored in this. So get yourself a decent size box that can keep the really important stuff - your end tackle.

Luggage wise, there are literally thousands of types. I use the expander carryall from Shimano, which like it says on the tin can expand considerably to take the kit needed for long sessions or kept smaller for shorter sessions. These are good when using a barrow. However if you want to carry your kit, then a 40litre rucksack is perfect to take enough kit for a session plus food! Once again stick to luggage from known brands such as Shimano and Trakker, you won't go far wrong.

The Fox box has a complete range of small accessory boxes, in one of these I keep my Safezone leadclips in a variety of colours so that I can match my lead arrangement to the lakebed type that I'm fishing on. If it's silty I'll use the dark silt coloured safezone ones, if it's a rocky bottom, then I'll use either the gravel lead clips or clay coloured ones depending on the tone of the lakebed. These might seem like small details, but they genuinely put extra carp on the bank. My 4 compartment box, has stick clips, Korda Kwik Links and silicon sleeves in. These are important components when PVA bag fishing and for quick tactical changes.

In another box I keep an array of swivels, link loops and ring swivels. These are all compatible with my Korda lead clips, which ensures fish safety. If you buy a pack of leadclips, ensure you buy the swivels from the same company, this guarantee's that everything fits correctly and means the rig will work properly and safely.

Other important items are boilie stops, I keep a small range of normal boilie stops and the excellent small and medium Extenda stops, which allows me to secure baits of different softness and texture with ease.

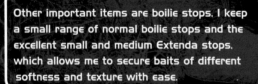

I also have a Tribal accessory pouch which I keep other larger items of end tackle in. During this book I cover various rigs that will require different hooklink materials. This is imperative when tying up rigs to suit different conditions. I keep a variety of hooklinks in my pouch, such as IQ Fluorocarbon, Supernatural braid, Hybrid soft coated braid, Bristle filament and Double Strength.

Lead size and shape plays a pivotal part in my angling for any species, a small adjustment in leadsize can turn twitchy bites into full blooded screamers! Korda Developments have always been the innovators and leaders in lead shape design and manufacturing. Every lead has a use and application and during this book we will visit some of these presentations. As a result I always carry an array of Korda leads to satisfy my presentation requirements.

Rig tools! Boilie needles, pulla tools and scissors are simple yet very important tools. To start with I would recommend you get a boilie needle, scissors and pulla tool for tightening knots. However as you can see I always carry the full range of tools, for use with different materials such as leadcore, braid and monofilament.

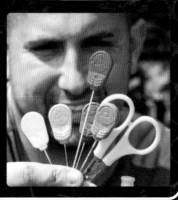

The single most important thing in any tackle armoury, HOOKS! It's the pivotal point of contact between one man and his dream fish! Don't skimp on these. I carry my favourite Korda hooks, because I trust them as being the sharpest and most expertly designed hooks on the market. I have different shapes and sizes to suit different rigs. I also change a hook after every fish, I learnt at a very young age, that the cost of a hook is a small price to pay for landing your target fish. Do not be lazy on this subject, trust me, losing a fish because you didn't change your hook is a risk not worth taking.

Spare Safezone leaders, ideal for beginners and experienced angler alike. Add your lead system, palomar knot your line to the small loop at the end of your safezone leader and you're ready to fish with a superb fast sinking camo leader. I keep spares of all colours similar to my lead clips in my carryall.

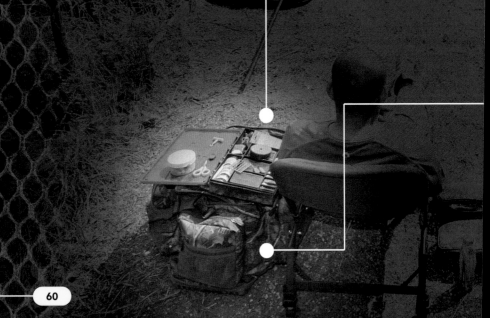

Always have a few pots of different hookbaits in your carryall. Small hookbait changes on any given session can make all the difference, bright ones, pellet shaped ones and plastic baits all have a place in my arsenal.

If you want to invest in a rod pod then go for it. I have always been a bit of a tackle tart and preferred the Stainless steel and stabiliser combination. I stare at my rods so much I want them to look handsome! Also buzzer bars and backrest bars are important when using multiple rod set-ups. Banksticks are perfectly adequate to start with, but if the lake you fish has hard banks, then go for a rod pod.

Hopefully it won't be too long before you're banking some big carp! If you get off to a good start, then invest in a weigh sling and scales! It's always nice to know how big the fish are that you're catching! However if you're tight on budget, just borrow the scales from the guy next door!

There are certain items that you just have to carry. You will see throughout this book just how instrumental PVA and the Funnel web systems are in my fishing. Things like PVA, hooks and consumables should always remain a priority on your shopping list. These are so crucial to consistent success, that placing these below flash rods and reels on your shopping list is denying you results in your angling.

Well there we have it, a whirlwind but brief look at the essentials that you will need for your fishing. Stick to top brands and quality products. It's a hobby so making expensive mistakes shouldn't be par for the course. Hopefully this has been informative and will help you make a few good decisions along the way.

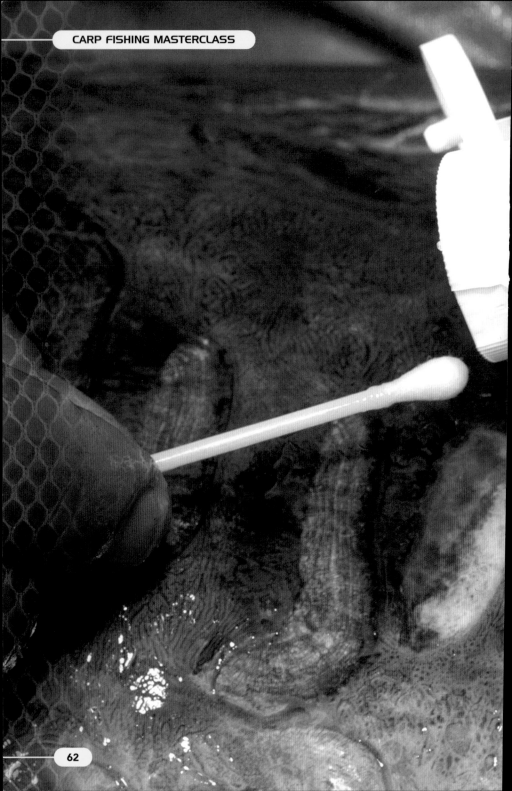

FISH CARE

It's all well and good showing you how to put extra carp on the bank, but it's no use catching them if you're going to harm them when your quarry is in the net. I have been horrified on a number of occasions when I have witnessed sub standard fish care on the bank. I've seen anglers on so called syndicate waters leave a fish on the carp mat so they can return to their vehicle and fetch the camera. Quite unbelievable acts of selfishness and ignorance when I think about it. I'm sure all of you out there would never intentionally harm a fish. At the end of the day, they give us so much joy, so looking after them on the bank and ensuring they go back in tip top shape is the least we can do.

This chapter is all about showing the simple principles that you should all follow when you get a carp in the net, to ensure they are transferred onto the bank and back into the drink in mint condition. The young spring chicken Tom Dove is super careful when he has fish on the bank and you should all follow his lead, so who better to demonstrate the procedure, than the dove from above, himself.

OI With the fish in the net, break the net down ensuring you have plenty of slack line coming off the rod and that the line is not tight leading to the hookhold. This ensures that the hook doesn't tear when lifting the fish out.

02

With the net folded down, and your weigh sling zero'd slip the weigh sling under the net. Do this all with the fish still in the water.

03

Now check that all fins are flat against the fish's body. Ensure that the pectoral fins are flat against the body of the fish, that the dorsal and anal fins are not stuck in the net holes. This is vital.

04

Slowly and carefully lift the fish out. Ensure you have a strong foot-hold. If it's too heavy get assistance.

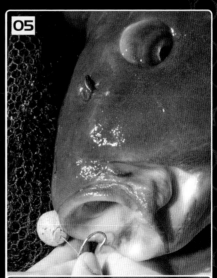

05

Carefully place the fish on the unhooking mat. Unfold the net and keep the fish wet at all times. Now gently pop the hook out. Don't pull or tear it, a push at the eye of the hook should be just enough.

06 Ensure you have water handy. Lift the fish up, using your legs as support, you look beautiful Mr Dove! Say cheese.

07

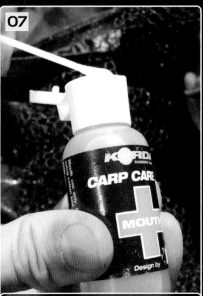

Before you return the fish, check the fish for any blemishes or cuts. The Carp Care Kit is brilliant at remedying these.

08

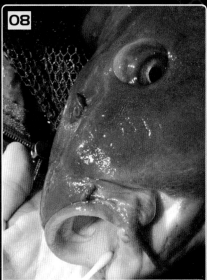

With the cotton bud provided and using the mouth, part of the Carp Care Kit apply the gel to hook holds or cuts in the carps mouth. This antiseptic gel really helps a speedy tissue recovery.

09

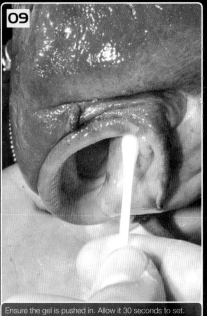

Ensure the gel is pushed in. Allow it 30 seconds to set.

10

Once again pour more water over the fish.

II

The Carp Care Kit also has a fluid to assist in the recovery of bodily cuts and sores.

I2

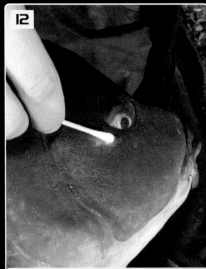

Dry the affected area and once again apply the body Carp Care Kit liquid. Allow to set for 30 seconds. Ensure you keep control of the carp at all times by covering its eyes and keeping your hands on the body.

I3

Gently lower the sling back into the water. Make sure you never lift a sling until the fins are flat against the fish's body.

I4

Keep one hand on the tail and another below the fish's tail and let it get its energy back.

15 When you feel the fish pulling and wanting to return, let go of the tail and let your prize swim happily free, no worse for its experience.

BOTTOM BAIT RIGS

In this chapter we're going to look at a simple bottom bait rig, that will serve you well from the word go. Always remember that complicated doesn't always mean better, and this certainly rings true with the rig that I'm covering in this chapter. Even for a self proclaimed beginner, these are a doddle to tie and should have you bent into carp on the bottom very soon!

THE DECISION PROCESS

The key thing a beginner needs to understand, and remember is that there is NO perfect rig. People often ask me what is my number one rig, what rig do I use when my head is on the 'chopping block'? That rig doesn't exist and the reason is simple. Lots of variables help me to decide what presentation I need to use. This means both adjustments to my hooklink and lead system.

So what are the variables? Lakebed, baiting strategy, bottom debris and hookbait choice all play a critical part in my thought process. In this chapter we're going to look at a couple of bottom bait rigs that will serve you well from the word go. The first thing you need to remember is that these don't need to be complicated. Even for the self-proclaimed beginner, these are a doddle to tie and any of you can be out there using one of the rigs covered in this chapter in no time at all.

The decision process for using a bottom bait is quite simple. If I'm using small seed baits or fishing over a clean firm bottom without the risk of masking my hookbait on bottom debris I will often opt for a bottom bait. However it's important to use freebies of different sizes. Why? Because if you feed one size of bait and then present a hook on one of these, then the hookbait will behave considerably differently to the freebies which could in turn alarm feeding carp that pick up the hookbait. The same goes for when fishing over particles. I won't use a 20mm sinking boilie if I'm presenting the bait over a bed of hemp or small 10mm boilies. The reason here again is simple, if fish are consistently picking up one size of bait that is very small, then a large bait over the top is going to be treated with caution. Fish often get preoccupied on beds of freebies, so your hookbait not only needs to be presented where they are feeding, it also needs to behave similarly to your loosefeed. If it doesn't, then even on a well stocked venue, the carp will smell a rat and more often than not neglect your hookbait.

Bottom baits over beds of bait are often a good choice because fish are feeding hard on the bottom and are used to sucking bait off the deck, as a result a pop-up wouldn't be the right choice here. Even in silt I still like bottom baits when fishing over beds of bait, because more often than not, fish have their heads buried in the stuff, often up to their gills, as they feed on your loose feed.

TIE THE CLAW RIG

If you want a rig that's easy to tie, but extremely efficient at converting feeding fish into fish on the bank then look no further. You won't be needing shrink tube or rig rings, just a bit of silicon tubing, a kurv shank hook and a coated braid!

01
The components required are a size 8 Kurv shank hook and a coated braid.

02
Strip back 4 inches of the coating from the hooklink material.

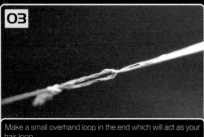
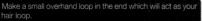
03
Make a small overhand loop in the end which will act as your hair loop.

04
Slide on a dumbbell shaped or standard shaped boilie.

05
Secure in place with a small extenda stop.

06
At the other end of the hooklink with the aid of a splicing needle thread on a 3mm length of 0.5mm silicon tubing.

07

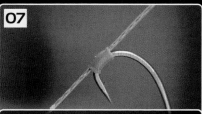

Carefully and slowly tease the hook point between the tubing and coated braid. Ensure that you push the hook through the silicon with the hook point facing down to the hookbait.

08

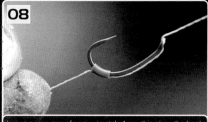

Leave a nice gap of approximately 1cm, this gives the hook and bait freedom for better hookholds.

09

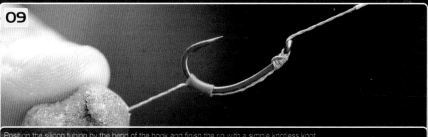

Position the silicon tubing by the bend of the hook and finish the rig with a simple knotless knot.

Bottom bait success whilst filming for Online Fishing TV

So think about the baiting situation and also the bottom make-up. Its also worth bearing in mind the physics and behaviour of a hook in water. A lot of people are obsessed with getting the hook to turn in the palm of their hand on the bank. However in water the hook will always hang down point first attacking the bottom lip of the fish. The reason for this is that the point area of the hook is the heaviest part of the hook. As a result, I always exit the hair from the bend of the hook when using a bottom bait.

This helps to increase the weight of the hook point even more, which in turn exaggerates the hooking capability of the bottom bait presentation. This can be achieved with a small amount of silicon tubing as shown in the picture sequence. It's such a small detail, but it will increase the efficiency of your presentation ten fold as a result.

The final point that you need to consider when choosing the right bottom bait presentation, is the right material for the right bottom. If the lakebed is very soft then you don't want a stiff hooklink as this will stick out the bottom at an angle and give you an ineffective presentation. On softer bottoms choose softer hooklinks such as braid or soft light mono's such as 10lb IQ. This will help your rig to pick up the contours of the lakebed. When using softer hooklinks, it's important to use PVA bags or stringers. This helps to eliminate tangles on the cast and ensures that your rig is sitting pretty.

Hopefully this whistle stop tour of bottom baits has cleared up some confusion. Like any rig, used in the right situations as covered in this chapter, bottom baits can be devastating.

An awesome mid-20 common which was a sucker for a bottom bait.

A BALANCING ACT

My fishing over the last 3-4 years has been tactically, dominated with the use of balanced baits. For many of you, the words 'balanced bait' won't mean a thing. So let me explain. A 'balanced bait', is a bait that just sinks under the weight of the hook. Bottom baits will normally sink at quite a pace to the bottom, whilst pop-ups sink at pace due to the weight of the shot, or slower if you use a smaller shot to pin the pop-up down.

However with any boilie it is possible to critically balance the presentation so it sinks ever so slowly to the lakebed. However there are other ways of doing it, and that is covered in the KD rig picture sequence, which has been my most successful rig over the last few years.

The reason that a 'balanced bait' is so effective is because the bait behaves like a free offering. The presentation is almost weightless, because the buoyancy of the bait negates the weight of the hook. Fish on pressured venues are not used to this. When the fish sucks up the hookbait, it flies into their mouth at the same speed as a free offering, which is a problem that they're not used to.
In my opinion this type of hookbait presentation is far more refined than a standard bottom bait, and more subtle than a pop-up, which can be the small tactical adjustment that one needs on a tricky day.

THE KD RIG

This is one particular presentation that I would happily use in a number of circumstances. It lends itself perfectly to single hookbait fishing. If you're new to a venue and on a short day-session, a fluoro boilie that has been critically balanced similarly to the KD rig in this feature can be an ideal starting approach. The critically balanced bottom bait sits hovering only a few millimetres off the bottom. Which still leaves it primed for inspection off a feeding carp. Also due to the behaviour of the bait and the way that it flies into the fishes mouth when sucked up, carp are less likely to eject the hookbait as it behaves similarly to the smaller food items such as hemp and corn.

I still recommend that whenever you fish particles, that you use various sizes, so that the fish find it a lot harder to distinguish between hookbait and free offering. This way a small (12mm-14mm) round balanced boilie, that is wafting around is still a deadly hookbait option over beds of particles.

What is also wonderful about this type of presentation, is that it lends itself expertly to being used over beds of boilies. Whether you catapult your bait in a close 'clump' or spread over a tennis court sized area, this presentation will always help to trip up wily carp. However another tip that I always give when I fish over boilies, is to introduce multiple sizes. So don't just feed 14mm baits or just 18mm baits, try introducing a mixture, because similarly to particle fishing, a variety of sizes does not allow the carp to become used to every bait, behaving exactly the same. Once again, this will mean that your hookbait will be under less scrutiny by pressured carp when it finally gets picked up.

TIE THE KD RIG

When my friends first saw me use the KD rig, many of them laughed at how silly it looks, "how on earth does that catch fish" they heckled! The only people that had the last laugh was my dear friend Tom Dove and I. In just a few years this rig has been championed by Tom and I, to the point that I can't believe just how many people use it now and how many fish its catching. It's not only simple to tie, but it's quite simply an outrageously good carp catcher. Tie it, use it and watch those alarms wail!

01 You will need a Kurv shank pattern of hook in either 6,8 or 10 and a supple braid like the Supernatural material.

02 Peel off about 15 inches of Supernatural.

03 Tie an overhand loop in one end of the braid, this will be your hair loop, then thread on your 14mm pop up boilie.

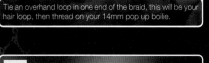

04 Secure the bait in place with a small Extenda stop.

05 Now thread the other end of the braid through the back of the eye.

06 Note the position of the bait before I tie the KD knotless knot. I like a 1mm gap between the top of the bait and the bend of the hook.

07

First wrap twice around the hook above the hair as shown.

08

Then continue to wrap under the hair a further 5 times, thus trapping the hair between the two wrapping points.

09

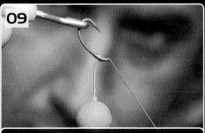

Fasten the knot tight with the aid of a Pulla tool.

10

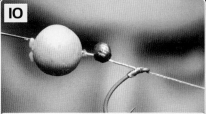
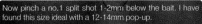

Now pinch a no.1 split shot 1-2mm below the bait. I have found this size ideal with a 12-14mm pop-up.

11

Peel over 3 inches of Kwik melt PVA tape.

12

Now use this to tie the hair tight to the bend of the hook, this will eliminate tangles during casts with this rig.

13

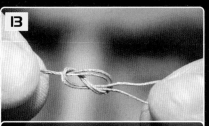

Tie a simple figure of eight loop knot in the other end of the braid. This will allow for quick changing of rigs.

14

Pour a small handful of stick mix into the original funnel web system.

15 Tie this off nice and tight.

16 Thread the bag onto a stringer needle

17 Thread the Funnel web bag onto the hooklink and carefully pull the hook into the groundbait in the bag.

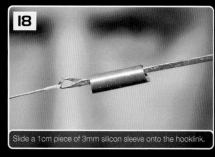

18 Slide a 1cm piece of 3mm silicon sleeve onto the hooklink.

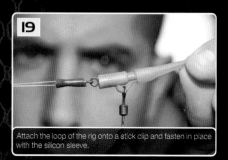

19 Attach the loop of the rig onto a stick clip and fasten in place with the silicon sleeve.

20 The finished rig is delicate, tangle proof and deadly! Get on it!

HOOKBAIT OPTIONS

Due to limited space, I have only touched on a few hookbait options. However the options are endless. I'm a big fan of plastic hookbaits and that's something that you will see elsewhere in this book. Due to the variety of plastic hookbaits that Enterprise Baits offer, you really are spoilt for choice. The size of them lends itself perfectly to critically balancing, and a small shot No4 or No6 is sometimes all you need to sink them ever so slowly.

Cork inserts into boilies and also bits of plastic maize/corn, to tip off standard boilies also help to add buoyancy to your hookbait, this will give it an added edge.

Using tubs of pop-ups and then either securing a shot to the hair so the bait just sinks is also another deadly method. Alternatively, thread the bait onto the hair and then slowly trim the bait with scissors. Keep testing it in the margins until the bait just sinks under the weight of the hook. Very simple to do, yet I very rarely see anyone doing it on any venue that I visit.

SUMMARY

As you can probably tell, this is a method that I really favour. It has put hundreds of big carp on the bank for me, and its not testimony to me, its credit to this method. It lends itself perfectly to fishing over a variety of baiting situations, but also for fishing over a variety of lakedbeds. Using a slow sinker or critically balanced bait, over silt or silkweed is a devastating method. Small adjustments like this really do make a difference. Also coupled with a PVA stick or bag and you have a perfect short session method. The rig covered is my take anywhere rig and 99/100 it's my starting approach on any new venue. If you make it yours, you won't go far wrong either.

A wily 55lb 5oz mirror carp. Another victim of the KD rig.

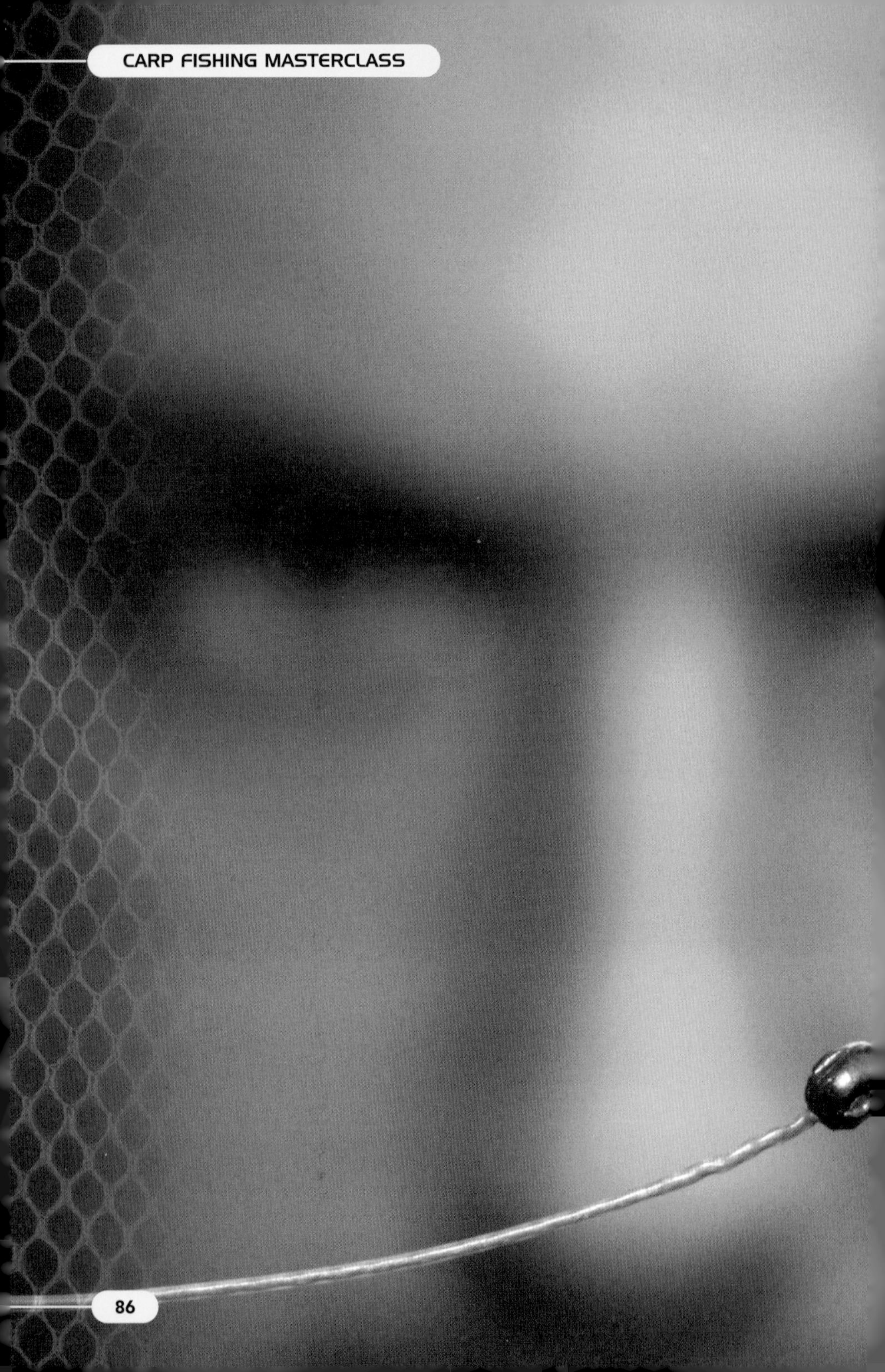

TOP OF THE POPS

This isn't something to be afraid of as much of the carps natural food sources are found in silt pockets. However to fish effectively in these conditions you need a rig that will present a bait effectively in front of the carps noses. The word 'pop-up' can scare some people and make them think that you need some super complicated rig to make your presentation work. Well the simple fact is that you don't. Carp rigs over the last few years have become focused heavily around making the hook turn and catch hold in the bottom lip of the carp.

In this chapter, we will be taking a look at a couple of pop-up rigs that can get you on your way and hopefully put a few bonus carp on the bank for you. I have used pop-ups ever since I started carp fishing back in the early nineties and I can safely say they have put numerous carp in my landing net as a result. When the chips are down and fishing is slow, a change over to a pop-up presentation can be the little tweak that your tactics need to convert lazy feeding carp into banked carp. However they are not always the correct choice of tactic, and like bottom bait fishing, there is always a time and a place.

SINGLE HOOKBAITS

On short sessions, a pop-up rig can be the ideal approach especially when coupled with a small 50pence size funnel web bag. Very often at the start of a session on a new water, I will initially start my day by casting single hookbaits to showing fish or areas that I think carp may frequent. Often I will use bright coloured hookbaits, which are high in flavour content and the lure of these are so strong, that they almost act like a scattering of lower flavoured boilies.

However, in this instance there is only one food item for them to eat and that's your hookbait. Please note, that I would never use over flavoured baits as freebies or loosefeed as these won't agree with the carps digestive system. Additionally due to the buoyant nature of the rig, it also keeps the hook above bottom debris, giving you peace of mind and ensuring that you're fishing as effectively as possible. Due to it being slightly elevated from the lakebed, it also sticks out a little more to roaming carp and can often be just enough to entice a bite from a carp that would be otherwise uninterested.

FISHING OVER WEED OR SILT

Pop-ups come into their own when fishing over detritus, debris or silkweed on the lakebed. A bottom bait cast onto such lakebeds risks the chance of being masked and deemed ineffective. Which in effect means you could be fishing for hours with your hook and hookbait completely encased in silkweed, which is as much use, as a chocolate tea-pot! Once again, any of the pop-up presentations that I have shown in this chapter will be adequate and suitable for combating this problem. If you feel that the weed is slightly heavier, but the carp are feeding in it, then use a light lead (1oz-1.5oz), a longer hooklink of 14inches or so and place the shot below the pop-up at 2-3 inches from the hook, which will ensure that your presentation sits pretty above the weed.

I like to test my pop-ups in the margins and choose the correct shot size or amount of putty to suit the bottom I'm fishing over. For example, if the lakebed I'm casting over is hard and gravelly, then I'll 'overshot' the pop-up so it sinks quickly to the bottom. However if I'm fishing over weed or silt, then I'll adjust the shot size or amount of putty on the rig so that the whole lot sinks very slowly. This will give you a critically balanced pop-up, which will rest perfectly over soft bottoms. By carrying a mixed tub of shot, you will be able to adjust your sinking time, to suit the size of pop-up and the lakebed that you're fishing over.

POP-UP OVER BAIT

This is the grey area that I get so many questions asked about. Fishing pop-ups over beds of small seeds like hemp or pellet can be a problem area. What you need to remember here is that you have the fish feeding hard on the bottom, and on soft bottoms, they even have their snouts deep into the lakebed. What this means is that a pop-up will often be ineffective when fish are feeding hard because the bait is past their mouths.

However, fishing beds of boilies, spread over a big area is a whole new ball game. When using boilies, carp will often tilt down and eat a bait, then lift their bodies up and swim around looking for the next one. You rarely get a 'hoovering' effect as they are feeding in a large area and this invariably means they are moving from boilie to boilie as they look for them. As a result a pop-up, which smells stronger and is off the lakebed can often be taken before all the freebies are wiped out. Often when I fish two or three rods over a bed of boiles, then I will fish one rod on a bottom bait and one on a pop-up. More often than not, the pop-up rod will be the first to go. So avoid using these in most instances over small particles, however when using boilies that match your hookbait size, then always try a pop-up over the top. It can often steal a bonus bite early in the session or when fish are not feeding too hard.

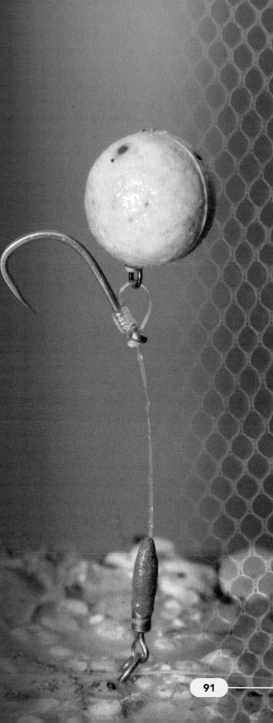

FLUOROCARBON POP-UP D-RIG

This is slightly more advanced as a rig, but still not that tricky to tie. With a bit of practice you should all be able to tie this up comfortably. It enables your pop-up to sit proud on the lake-bed, ready to snare feeding carp. Give it a go.

Here I'm using IQ2 in 10lb ES, a size 10 Kurv shank and small rig rings.

Take off about 15 inches of 10lb IQ2.

Begin to tie the knotless knot, but whip down level with the point of the hook.

Once you've done that whip back up over the barrel of the knot 3 times, this helps to secure the knot during a protracted fight on a light hooklink.

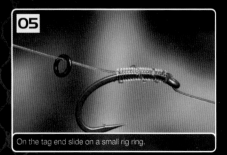

On the tag end slide on a small rig ring.

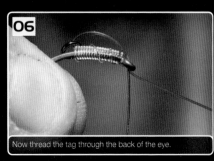

Now thread the tag through the back of the eye.

07

Pull it all the way through then begin blobbing with the lighter. You want to blob it so you have about 3-4mm protruding from the front of the eye.

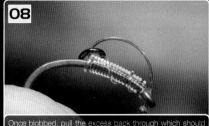

08

Once blobbed, pull the excess back through which should leave you with a lovely formed 'D'.

09

Take off a length of dental floss.

10

About 5 inches should be ample.

11

Thread the floss through the rig ring.

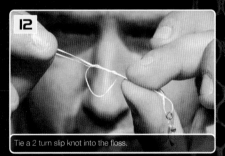

12

Tie a 2 turn slip knot into the floss.

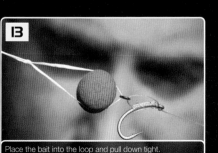

13

Place the bait into the loop and pull down tight.

14

Once tight, tie a few granny knots into the slip knot with the tag ends, cut off and blob with a lighter to tidy it all up. Add a split shot that will sink the pop-up slowly about 1-2 inches from the hook.

THE EASY RIG

If the pop-up rig on the previous page was a bit too complicated for you, then this set-up should be just the 'kiddy'. I know many big fish anglers that will cast a rig like this on any water in the land, confident that it will hook and land their target fish.

01 Two components are all you need, a pack of Wide Gape hooks and some Supernatural braid.

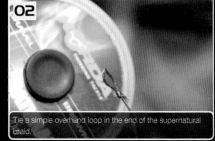

02 Tie a simple overhand loop in the end of the supernatural braid.

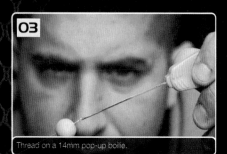

03 Thread on a 14mm pop-up boilie.

04 Secure in place with a small extenda stop.

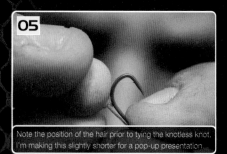

05 Note the position of the hair prior to tying the knotless knot. I'm making this slightly shorter for a pop-up presentation.

06 Complete the knotless knot like so.

Always carry a mixed tub of split shot so that you can balance your pop-ups perfectly.

Squeeze one on that will sink your pop-up slowly, and you're ready to go.

CONCLUSIONS

This should have given you a quick overview of pop-up fishing and really get you on the road to getting the best out of them. The rigs I have covered are simple to tie and more than adequate to get you started and understanding just how effective pop-up fishing can be when used in the right situation. On today's session at Cemex's Stanford-le-Hope Fishery, I have been fishing over quite heavy silk weed and silt, yet the pop-up rigs have been presented beautifully over the top resulting in numerous bites. The bright Plum and Mainline Pineapple pop-ups that I have been using coupled with the small Funnel web bags have been all that I needed to fool the carp, resulting in an action packed day. It just goes to prove once again, that on short sessions you can't beat a bright pop-up.

ZIG RIGS

Just the word 'zig' immediately puts people off fishing this immensely successful style of angling. People think it's too complicated or that it takes some ultra-specialist rig to catch using it. Well quite frankly these are all myths. So what is a 'zig rig'? In very simple terms it is the slightly bizarre name given to a rig that is suspended from the weight off the bottom with the aid of a buoyant hookbait. The weight acts as an anchor whilst the hookbait sits suspended in the water column trying to catch fish that are swimming in the other layers of water above the bottom.

It's hard to explain just how successful this method is, but on many summer days or even winter this can turn fishless days into action packed 'red letter days'. So why is this? Carp do not just feed on the bottom as many of you will know. Additionally when they are not on the top, it doesn't necessarily mean they are on the bottom. Fish can spend long periods during high-pressure days sitting and feeding in more comfortable mid water levels. Carp react to air pressure. When you are faced with low pressure (wet, cloudy, windy days), fish will happily feed on the bottom, however in the summer/early autumn, these days are few and far between. High pressure comes hand in hand with hot sunny days. This means that fish are reluctant to spend their time low in the water. To catch carp beyond float casting range, you need to use a simple method that can help you capitalise on this, and a 'zig' does exactly that. To help demonstrate this style of fishing we are focusing a day at Layer pits in Colchester, Essex. Ironically this was the water that some 14 years back I learnt to 'zig rig' fish on, so where better to prove how devastating this

method can be. However when I woke up this morning I chuckled at how cloudy and rainy the weather was, almost the opposite conditions to what I would recommend 'zig rig' fishing in. Nonetheless I was determined to prove how good this tactic is and decided to persevere with my initial plans.

Layer Pits isn't your normal club water. It belongs to Colchester Angling Preservation Society (CAPS). However this venue is steeped in carp fishing and match fishing history. It's huge stocks of double figure and 20lb carp have made it the birthplace of some very successful angling tactics over the last 25 years. Dinger Hum was just a regular club angler and he went on to develop the 'big waggler' method, which involved fishing just under the surface with a single caster or a couple of maggots and catching huge bags of carp as they rose up for the 'little and often' catapults full of maggots and groundbait in the upper water layers. Carp on this venue went crazy for this little and often baiting strategy, which meant they spent most of their time attacking baits on the surface. A float with a small 6-12" drop was catching fish after fish on the drop! Since then this method has evolved and today we are blessed with having the likes of the 'bagging waggler' in our angling armoury thanks to that original little gem.

Once again it was on this water that two famous angling twins the 'Messengers' (Neil & Darren) perfected a method that they had invented on wait for it....Zyg Gregoreks Angling paradise venue. Hence the name 'zig rig'. The method is so simple to tie and use, as the picture sequence shows, that it shocks me that more anglers do not use it. Follow the step-by-steps and you will not go far wrong. As a result I first picked up on this style of angling in the early 90's during my carp fishing scholarship so to speak. On many days it was impossible to get a bite on anything else other than zig rigs. It shocked me that so many of the more experienced anglers would just sit there waiting for nothing to happen, or doing nothing but sit there waiting for the cooler summer evening breeze to set in, which meant they might catch a fish off the bottom! Without trying to sound like a 'big head', I was 'having it off' on 'zigs' along with my mates, while others would catch nothing! That eye-opener was enough to engrain zig rigs in my angling 'skill-set' forever.

ZIG LEAD SET-UP

Lead size is pivotal when zig rig fishing. Use the smallest lead that you can get away with, which can still get you out to the range that you want to fish at. Because you have so much line between the lead and hook, you want to produce a good direct contact with your hook. With big leads you just end up playing the lead and not the fish.

01

For fishing at 60-80yds, I use nothing more than a 2oz lead.

02

Firstly cut the swivel on the lead off with a set of pliers or wire cutters.

03

The finished job will look like this, with the swivel cut off and the brass loop intact.

04

Because the long hooklink of the zig can be so tangle prone, you need to use a helicopter style set-up. By using the Korda helicopter leader you do not have the hassle of making your own DIY version. This is safe and easy to use straight out of the packet.

05

Simply take the leader out of the packet and it comes complete with all the required beads, Kwik Links and swivels.

06

Simply hook the brass loop of the lead onto the metal tail of the Kwik Link and slide the sleeve down.

THE ZIG RIG

There is mothing complicated about this method at all. Anglers think you need some crazy hard to tie set-up. The truth is the rig couldn't be simpler to tie. An easy knotless knot and you're away.

OI

Zig rigs are not complicated to tie, but your components need to be good, I use what is in my eyes the sharpest and most reliable hook on the market, the Korda Wide Gape in Size 10, and also the king of floater and zig rig hooklinks; Drennan Double Strength. Today I'm using 12lb BS, but on other venues with smaller fish I will use anything down to a 6lb BS.

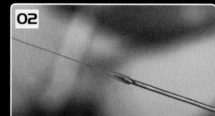

02

Firstly make a small overhand loop at the end of your line which will act as the tag end of your hair.

03

Now using a measuring device, like the one on top of a tackle box or Rig Safe, measure the length of hooklink that you require. For a 7ft zig I will measure off about 7.5ft to compensate for knots reducing the length of line.

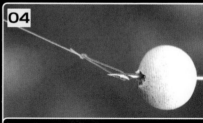

04

Now pull your hookbait onto the hair with your boilie needle.

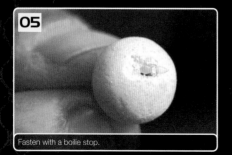

05

Fasten with a boilie stop.

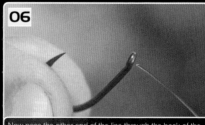

06

Now pass the other end of the line through the back of the hook eye. This is the start of the knot-less knot.

07

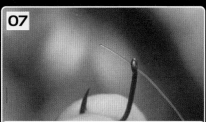

Ensure it goes through the back otherwise you will negatively affect the hooking efficiency of the hair rig.

08

Pull the rest of the line through until the boilie at the other end is about 2mm below the bend of the hook. This keeps the bait nice and tight to the hook, but still gives the hook enough movement away from the hair to catch hold in the carp's mouth.

09

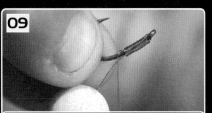

Now whip the line around the hook until it is level with the barb of the hook. Approx 1mm below the hook point on a standard size 10 hook.

10

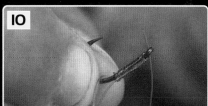

Now pass the line back through the back of the eye (yes all 7ft of it!). This completes the knotless knot. Now pull the knot tight, bed all the coils in and take the stretch out of the knot.

11

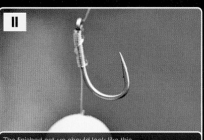

The finished set-up should look like this.

12

The final piece in the zig-saw is one of the Korda anti-tangle sleeves. Thread this onto the end of the hooklink with the narrow end going on first.

13

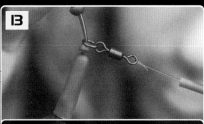

Now simply tie your Zig rig to your helicopter lead arrangement.

14

As previously mentioned, all you have to do now is tie your leader to your mainline with a Palomar knot. I tend to do this before putting the hooklink on as the Palomar knot can be completed with far more ease.

So how do you go about fishing this method? It's really simple. I like to find the depth of water that is in front of my swim. Today I'm using a marker float set-up, this tells me exactly how deep the water is in front of me. If I'm fishing closer in and want to change from a float set-up to a more static ledger zig set-up, then I will plumb the depth and fish the zig at different levels in the water. On today's trip I have 9ft of water at the 60yds range that I'm fishing. I have tied my rigs exactly as shown in the picture sequence and they have been tied to the lead set-up at 7.5ft and 5ft. This gives me two different options for intercepting the fish. Generally I favour the length of the 'zig' to be about 1.5ft below the surface, however on every session I will start with different lengths just in case they don't want to come right up to the surface to feed on the loose feed that is dropping down through the water column. If one rod is producing fish straight away and the other is either catching less or nothing, then a new rig will be quickly tied and set at the depth of the one which is producing the goods.

Once you have cast your baits to areas that you are happy with, commence your baiting approach. The picture sequence will show you my favoured type of bait. I will then introduce my bait little and often, so that I can stimulate some competitive feeding on the surface and in the upper layers of the lake. Today I'm using the Korda Skyliner spod to get my 'soupy' spod mix out to my marked area where my two baits are being fished. Often on high pressure, hot sunny days, your only true consistent chance of success will be on zig rigs! Fish are reluctant to feed with any intensity on the bottom, which makes them harder to catch. The surface however is a completely different ball game. Carp enjoy being in the upper layers, and that constant trickle of baits with different buoyancies will have them excitedly chasing baits up and down the water column. By using the cloudy mix that I have highlighted, you create a tantalising cloud of attraction that sits suspended in the upper 3-4 feet of water. This 'bubble' of attraction sends the carp crazy and keeps them searching for something slightly more edible in the upper layers, and because my mix has very small food items in it, they only have your hookbait as an appetising larger food source!

THE SOUPY SPOD MIX

Making the soupy spod mix can be quite fun, but also inexpensive and easy. The key is colours, smell and achieving the cloud effect to keep the fish occupied as long as possible.

The key ingredients for my spod mix, you will develop your own favourites.

In a small mixing bucket, first add around 2 pints of ready cooked aniseed hemp from Bait tech. I tend to keep knocking up fresh mini batches of spod mix throughout the day rather than one big batch!

Next I add some Bait-Tech mixed partimix, approx 2 pints again.

I then give this lot a big mix up.

Next comes my ever faithful Mainline Response Pellets, in 3mm or 5mm, these really are the business and get the fish going mad.

Then comes our ever faithful sweetcorn. I add about 1/2pint to the mix.

07

Next comes the groundbait. First in, is my crushed hemp favourite. Mainlines Hemp Method and Bag mix, this gives me some small bits of hemp and a lovely sweet smelling element to my spod soup.

08

I then add a super successful groundbait: Black Silly bait.

09

Next comes the Ringers fishmeal Carp mix groundbait, and any bait used by Steve ringer can't be that bad can it??! I've used about 3 pints of groundbait in all.

10

Give the whole lot a big mix and it should look like this.

11

Next comes the icing on the cake, a big dosing of the Bait Syrup from Mainline. Any of the flavours are good, but my two favourites are tiger or coconut milk. Lace this into the mix.

12

Your mix should look like this now, sticky and absolutely oozing in attraction!

13

Now all you are left to do is add lake water until the spod mix is like a stodgy soup. 'Gloopy' and 'sticky' is the best description I can give.

14

The mix will sit heavy and smelly in the spod!

15

On landing in the water the spod will kick out a small cloud straightaway which is often visible from the bank.

16

Within a few seconds the cloud will become far more dramatic and the cloud of attraction will start to sink through the water column.

Just look at the cloud this lets off, with sinking and floating food particles. Amazing.

To the untrained eye the 'zig' has nothing going for it. It is hard to cast because, depending on how deep the water is in front of you, it can mean using hooklengths of anything, between 3-20ft (Just put the rig in an empty bucket coiled up, and away you go)! People can't get their head around a length of line protruding from the lake-bed with a buoyant bait on the end just wafting around in mid-water, how can that work they wonder?

Well it works beyond belief and I could have a wager with all of you, that on high-pressure summer days it will out-fish bottom bait tactics considerably. During today's session, the weather has been fantastic for catching them off the bottom, however due to the continued warm weather the fish are still starved of oxygen meaning that the likelihood is that they will be caught on the zigs. My results throughout the day proved this theory correct. Whilst anglers all around the lake were fishing with bottom baits, I wholeheartedly attacked it on zigs, and after a couple of hours the fish reacted to the baiting pattern and the takes started. Everyone else's alarms stayed silent with only the odd bite coming out elsewhere! Ignore zig rigs at your peril.

LEAD-ING THE WAY

Such a subtle object, such a forgotten object and often overlooked item of tackle. For many newcomers to carp fishing, the lead is probably only seen as a component that helps you get your bait, hook and rig to the bottom of the lake? BUT boy, it's so much more. In the minefield that is the lead market, it's very easy to walk into a shop, pick up any old shape and weight, pay your money and then leave. However what if I told you that your lead choice is as important as the rig you use in some circumstances.

I wonder how many of you realise JUST how important lead size and shape is in helping put more carp on the bank? Like me, many of you will be fishing pressured day ticket venues, where the fish have become accustomed to dealing with leads of average sizes. Its not so important on huge under stocked venues with big carp, it literally effects YOU and the waters you're fishing.

Over the next three chapters I'm going to be taking a close look at different lead shapes and colours, whilst explaining their properties and the where and when to use scenarios and then we will progress to the exact breakdown of different lead systems, so that you can couple your lead knowledge with lead systems. You can then ensure you're using the right system in the right conditions for perfect presentation and hooking efficiency every time.

TOURNAMENT CASTING SWIVEL LEAD

If you're looking for a lead for distance casting then this is the one. Due to its tapered nature, it is streamlined and aerodynamic in flight, allowing you to cast further than shorter squat shaped leads. Frank Warwick who was partly involved in the re-birth of this lead shape 10 years or so ago also felt that this shape is not as likely to penetrate into deep silt. Due to fishing a lot of silty mere's, he found retrieving this shape from the lake bed was a lot easier than other shapes with a heavy nose that allows the lead to penetrate deeper into the silt. So for an aerodynamic long distance casting shape, the Tournament casting would be my choice.

SWIVEL DISTANCE

This lead is the brainchild of Alan Partridge an 'Old School' angler well known in the higher echelons of carp fishing for his innovative thinking and his long range casting. He had ridiculed Danny Fairbrass for years saying 'my leads cast further than yours' so one day Danny bit and said 'go on then, prove it'. So the two of them went over to a local big pit and Danny cast as far as he could with his original slender and pointed Distance Casting lead, the slack was taken out and an elastic band was fitted tightly around the line before the lead was wound in. Danny's lead was taken off the lead clip and Alan's was put on. Danny again gave it the big un and pulled the elastic band straight off the spool plus about 30 yards of line!

To add insult to injury Alan allowed Danny to put his style of lead back on and see if he could hit the elastic, try as he might Danny could not match the distance, so he had to use Alan's design which has remained the same to this day! This lead shape is very streamlined and stable in flight. It doesn't wobble like some other distance shapes, and delivers your rig exactly where you aim. This is the shape I like for my distance fishing and along with the tournament lead design, you have two excellent shapes that will cater for your long distance work. The Tournament shape is probably more suited when fishing into deeper silty area's, whilst the distance swivel with its heavy nose design will help you cast to those unreachable targets!

FLAT SWIVEL PEAR

This is one of my favourite lead shapes for fishing on hard bottoms. The short condensed shape of this lead coupled with the two flat sides makes it the perfect lead for bolt rigs at short to medium range. By its very nature the flat pear lead lends itself to being fished on marginal slopes, the sides or back of gravel bars and in rivers. However I like to use this short squat shape for a lot of my short to medium range work. An accomplished caster can use this for fishing up to 100 yards. Like all the leads covered in this chapter, it has beautiful rounded edges, which helps to eliminate tangles.

Also with its flat edges, you have a more condensed weight which I believe aids hooking efficiency. Additionally the last thing you want on a flat bottom is your rig kicking up from a lead, this shape helps to eliminate this, and gives you a very flat and effective presentation. Of all the lead shapes available this is the one that most resembles a piece of gravel on the lakebed. An excellent hard bottom lead, that gives you prompt lead to hook weight transfer and excellent hooking efficiency. I like this in big sizes for margin work, and will think nothing of using a 5oz version when trying to fool cute pressured fish from under my rod tip. The condensed shape and heavy weight can be just the catalyst that you need to turn a fruitless session into a fruitful one.

SWIVEL PEAR

The classic pear lead will cast a very long way, almost as far as the Distance Casting and it is less affected by cross winds because the shape is very condensed. The dumpy shape can be used to your advantage in silt, try using a very light pear lead say 1oz or 2oz and actually let the lead plug into the silt, this will dramatically increase the resistance to a moving carp so what feels like a light lead in your hand is transformed into a heavy lead in the fishing situation. Because the lead has a large rounded end it makes 'feeling' the lead hit the bottom easier than more slender or pointed shapes. If you're getting used to feeling the lead down, this will make it a lot easier and allow you to feel 'the drop' with more sensitivity. If you look at many of the chod rig fanatics like Terry Hearn, then very frequently you will see them using this very lead shape. A very popular shape and design.

THE 'BIG GRIPPA'

This design is arguably the most popular lead design on the continent for people approaching large European reservoirs and snaggy lakes like Rainbow lake.

As it says on the tin, this lead shape is ideal when needing to grip the bottom with ease. It has been proven that a 1oz Grippa gives you as much grip as a 2oz swivel pear lead. So it's twice as effective in holding the bottom. This is what makes this lead a popular choice with barbel and river anglers in general. Because of its availability in 6,8,10oz, it is also the 'numero uno' for extreme fishing at range when using boats. Therefore for boat fishing, or when looking to ensure your rig is gripping bottom, there is no better option on the market.

THE SWIVEL SQUARE PEAR

The Underwater DVD's by Korda have played a pivotal part in the development of a lot of tackle items and were the inspiration behind this unique lead shape. Dan and the Korda team observed the reaction of fish during Underwater part 4. What needed to be achieved, was a lead shape that could provide the same hooking efficiency as an inline lead. With an inline lead, fish always hit the heaviest part of the lead first when the hooklink is straightened which heightens the chance of a hooked fish. To achieve the same result you need a condensed shape. The best at the time was the ball shape lead, however this is prone to rolling on a hard bottom, which isn't ideal. As a result the square pear was born.

With its flat sides and tapered edges you have a very squat shape that gives you an even load compressed into a small surface area. As a result the fish feels the full weight of the lead far quicker than it would with a Tournament swivel lead. Obviously its not as aerodynamic as the distance leads, however it is suitable for fishing comfortably up to 80-90 yards. Due to the shape it means you can use lighter leads, because they pack more punch. Similarly to the flat pear, I love this shape for fooling 'riggy' pressured carp. This is one shape that will definitely put more fish on the bank from difficult heavily fished venues.

INLINES

These have seen somewhat of a rebirth in my fishing during the last few years. I have approached a couple of pressured venues and felt that the extra hooking prowess of an inline would be more beneficial. Inlines are excellent, because when a fish sucks in the hookbait and straightens your hooklink, it feels the full weight of the lead quicker. This is due to the hooklink exiting directly out of the heaviest part of the lead. With a swivel lead, the whole lead needs to be lifted before the fish feels the full fury of the weight!

Inlines are ideal when fishing over hard to firm bottoms, however they are not so suited to fishing in deep silt or weed. As the hooklink exits from the nose of the lead, it has a tendency to charge into the silt or weed thus dragging your hooklink in with it, which in turn can ruin your presentation. If I do ever use inlines in weed or silt then I will do so whilst using a soft hooklink like Supernatural braid or a soft coated braid.

I have already covered most of the swivel shapes ,which are also available in an inline version, all the same principles are relevant however an inline generally will not cast as far as a swivel lead.

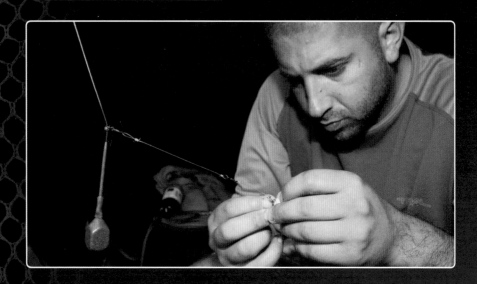

FLATLINER DISTANCE

One lead shape that is unique to the inline range is the Flatliner distance. This is a very aerodynamic shape, which lends itself to fishing over a firm bottom. Due to the raised nose of the lead, it also provides a very free pivot point for the hooklink. With its four flat sides, it will also land flush on one side, when fishing over hard bottoms. This will keep the lead 'still', ready to nail a wily carp.

COLOURS AND COATINGS

The world seems to have gone textured lead mad in the last few years, leads with manure and wood chip on them and white sand?? What's that all about? It has certainly caught a lot of anglers, but I doubt it has put any more fish on the bank for the users. In most instances I would say it has potentially cost people fish. A lot of people are so engrossed in this 'cult' looking lead, but its not what it looks like in the tackle shop, its what it looks like in water that matters!

Both Danny Fairbrass and I spent hours filming different leads underwater and I'm sure we will one day divulge this footage. The viewing is shocking. The leads pictured here are without a shadow of doubt the most camouflaged on the lakebed and are the nearest to resembling something that might appear on the lakebed. When fishing in clear lakes, it normally means fishing over gravelly bottoms. I don't see too many pebbles or shingle that resembles a 'dung bomb'! Even though some leads might have a shiny finish on the tackle shop shelf, doesn't mean they will look like that underwater. All the leads I have covered are the most camouflaged leads I have ever seen and I have filmed almost every type underwater.

Some of the bright green leads and coated leads look shocking. The 'texture' collects bubbles and sticks out like a sore thumb. As a result I will continue to use the 'flecked' coating like these, safe in the knowledge that I have the most camouflaged lead available today.

ALL SYSTEMS GO

Similarly to lead shape, the actual lead system that an angler chooses to use is very underestimated. It can have a massive impact on your results. If you make the right choice, you'll enjoy great sessions, but if you get it wrong, its very likely that you'll be sat behind motionless indicators, whilst watching carp putting on a sea-life centre 'display' in front of you. The thought process like anything in carp fishing is easy, as long as you know how. Over the next couple of chapters, I'll help to guide you in the right direction when faced with different lakebeds on any lake and swim.

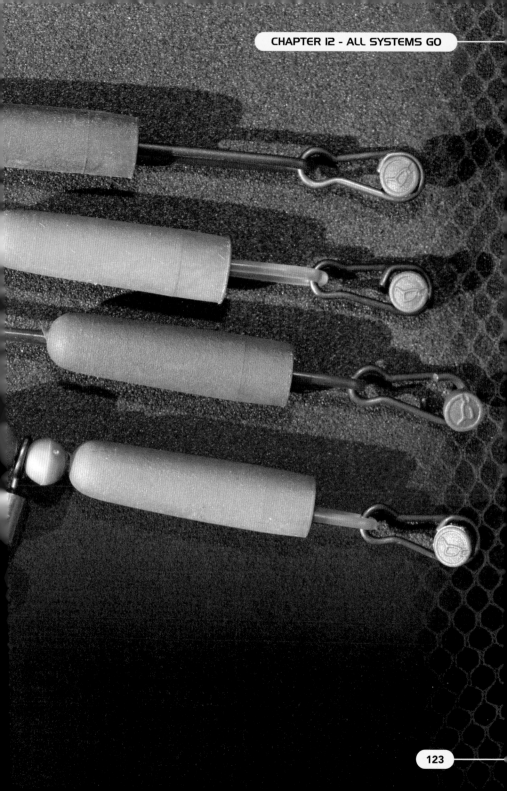

CRITICAL FACTOR

In the last chapter you would have seen a typical theme rising when describing lead shapes? The theme which, dictated lead choice, was lakebed make-up and rig efficiency. Choosing the right lead system is no different. In this chapter we are looking at two very popular systems, but like anything, there's a time and a place.

THE LEAD CLIP

This is arguably the most common lead system that is used by so many anglers. However like anything it's not always the number one choice for every situation. The lead clip evolved hugely when Danny Fairbrass re-vamped earlier design attempts by other companies. He created an inner ridge which helped a size 8 swivel or ring swivel to clip into place, ensuring that the lead clip stayed lodged on the swivel during casting and playing fish. For a streamlined casting system you really can't beat a lead clip. With a big-eyed swivel on the lead it sits beautifully on the arm of the clip, finding its home on the widest part of the arm. This allows the lead to hang parallel to the hooklink, which not only means it flies truly through the air, letting the lead shape achieve maximum distance, it also helps to eliminate tangles.

This is not always the case with braided hooklinks and single hookbaits, however with a coated braid such as Hybrid soft or mono hooklinks, it is a tangle proof lead system. Adding a PVA stringer or Funnel web bag to the hook area further ensures tangle free fishing. What is also great about a lead clip is its versatility. It is suited to almost all fishing situations.

THE LEADCLIP SYSTEM

Even though the lead clip has been around now for a very long time, I still see it used incorrectly or badly. When set-up properly, it is both safe and streamlined, helping to eliminate tangles and ultimately discharging the lead should it ever become snagged in weed or other water found hazards.

01

You will need a Safezone ring swivel leader matched to the lakebed you are fishing over, a Safezone lead clip and tail rubber once again matched to the lakebed and your leader.

02

Give the leader a stretch between your hands. This will take out any kinks in the leader and make it supple during use.

03

Thread your tail rubber onto your mainline.

04

Repeat the process with the lead clip.

05

With the aid of a palomar knot, tie your mainline to your leader.

06

Wet the ring swivel, this will help to click the lead clip in place.

07

Carefully pull the lead clip down your mainline and onto your leader. In one motion pull the swivel into the body of the clip so it CLICKS.

08

Note the 3mm silicon covering the swivel on the lead.

09

Pull the lead onto the arm of the leadclip.

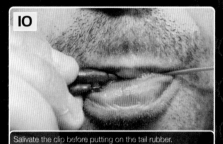

10

Salivate the clip before putting on the tail rubber.

Note how the tail rubber is only pushed over 2/3 teeth on the clip. The further you push the tail rubber on, the less chance you have of getting rid of the lead should a fish become snagged. BE SENSIBLE.

CLIPS IN WEED

When fishing in weed, I will couple the set-up with a small lead of 1-2oz, or as small as I can get away with to reach my required spots. Additionally, I position the tail rubber, so that it only covers 2 or 3 teeth on the outer bore of the clip. Ensure that you salivate under the tail rubber, and this will guarantee the lead coming off on the take, when fishing in weed. This is a small price to pay when you're angling for your dream fish. By ramming the tail rubber right down the clip, you are deeming this set-up ineffective in weed. Of course you will get a take or two, but the lead is unlikely to discharge which means you give a big surface area for weed to grab hold of, making it very difficult to bring fish back through weed. Even when fishing over clear areas or on weed free venues, please do not ram the tail rubber on, because if you ever 'crack off' the likelihood is that fish will pick up 'live' rigs and inevitably be trailing your rig and lead, which really puts our beloved quarry in danger of becoming tethered. One final tip for using them in weed; sometimes I even cut the arm down on the lead clip, and push the tail rubber up against the arm (so not even covering it), this gives the lead an even greater chance of coming off immediately when a fish bolts off.

Like any rig where the hooklink is not attached directly to the lead, it means the lead has a chance of penetrating into soft bottoms, but still enabling the hooklink to sit above shallow silt or silk-weed. This gives this system a major advantage over a standard inline set-up. The lead-clip is a good all round set-up and I would almost describe it as the 'jack-of-all trades' lead system. It's good at most things, however more specialist set-ups can be created when fishing over different lake-beds and situations. However if you're looking for a lead system that will perform in most situations, then the lead clip system that we have covered in this chapter will suit your fishing.

THE HELICOPTER/CHOD LEAD SYSTEM

The helicopter has been around for donkeys years now, but in recent times it has seen a bit of a rebirth via the nationwide use of the chod rig. Even though the 'choddy' as it has become affectionately known, centres around a short 2-3 inch pop-up hooklink, the lead system itself is very adaptable and well worth explaining. The word 'chod' is used to describe silt and detritus that is found on the lakebed. Having done a lot of fishing in the northwest, 'chod' was a big issue.

The helicopter rig itself is very aerodynamic and casts well. It was very popular due to its anti-tangle properties back in the nineties. However since then its performance on silty venues has carved it a new niche. Due to the lead entering the water first and being on the end of the line so to speak, it is the first thing to touch-down on the lake-bed. As you can imagine, with a lead-clip system or inline set-up, the lead is likely to drag the hooklink into deep silt as it penetrates, which in some instances can deem your presentation useless.

HELICOPTER / CHOD RIG

For peace of mind when fishing in deep chod / silt, you really can't beat this set-up. It's adjustable and adaptable, allowing you to present a bait effectively in difficult circumstances.

01

The Safezone helicopter/chod leader comes complete with everything that you need to set this rig up correctly.

02

Once the leader is out of the packet, give it a good stretch to take out any kinks.

03

The leader has a Kwik Link on it for easy lead attachment.

04

Take a lead of your choice and cut off the swivel so you are left with just the stainless loop.

05

It should look like so.

06

Now connect it to the leader via the Kwik Link.

07

Pull down the helicopter sleeve to make it neat and tidy.

08

You can now fish it like this which is an orthodox helicopter set-up.

09

Safezone leader's come ready finished with tungsten fused onto them. These are slightly greater in diameter than the main leader which means they safely hold a helicopter bead on them.

10

By moving the top bead onto the furthest tungsten collar from the lead, you now have a chod set-up allowing your hooklink to slide up and buff up against the top bead as the lead penetrates into silt.

With the 'choddy' the lead lands first. Because you have your hooklink swivel running on the Safezone leader, this then sits perfectly above the bottom debris, as the bore in the swivel gives enough room for the leader to pass through as its dragged into silt! How far the lead can travel before it drags your hooklink in, depends on the top buffer bead on your safe-zone leader. If the lake you are fishing only has a small surface layer of detritus, then put the buffer bead on the first tungsten fuse nearest the lead end, however, if you think its quite deep silt, then place the heli-bead on the 2nd tungsten fuse furthest away from the lead. This will help aid your presentation.

When using this presentation, you can get away with lovely short pop-up presentations such as the chod rig because of the behaviour of the rig, however if you use a bottom bait presentation, then try to use longer hooklinks of 8-12inches so that you don't risk your presentation hanging 'funny' if your leader lifts off the bottom due to an uneven lakebed. This system is great in weed-free silty lakes, however if you do use it on a weedy lake, then please either use a small lead, or attach the lead to the kwik link at the bottom of the leader with a 'weak link' of 4-6lb line. This will mean you get the same presentation qualities, but if the lead gets snagged, the line holding the lead to the link will snap, allowing you to have a true contact with the fish. All in all a great presentation for silty venues.

ALRESFORD FISHERY
Near Colchester, CO7 8JB

The newly opened CEMEX Angling day ticket water is a haven for the all round angler.

Featuring four fantastic lakes set in breathtaking scenery this venue is set to be one of the country's top complexes.

Jerry's lake is stocked with over 300 carp, some in excess of 25lb. Hall's lake for the pleasure / match angler is mainly tocked with bream and tench but also contains perch, chub, roach, rudd and crucians.

Ellis Pit, around 1 acre is set aside from the rest of the site, holding tench in excess of 8lb and crucians topping the 2lb mark. Jack's lake is the specimen lake where you can be lucky enough to catch hand-picked stunners including Leney - Dinks and pure strain Italians, the latest catch report is a fish of 28lb+.

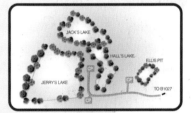

RUNNING AWAY

Having discussed two semi-fixed systems in the previous chapter, namely the lead clip and helicopter, I felt that it would be helpful to discuss some more sensitive setups for cuter carp – with regards to bite detection and rig ejection. Many carp anglers use one particular arrangement for all of their angling. I'm not saying that this is wrong but with a little thought and application with your lead system, you could catch extra fish. We've seen it time and time again having viewed the way that a carp feeds right in front of the camera on our popular underwater films.

At times, they actually use the whole weight of the lead to eject the hook. We've even witnessed them rise from the lake bed with the whole rig in their mouth only to sling it around the swim using the weight to set the hook free. You'll get 'done' time and time again as these cunning carp outfox your presentation. Eventually, you will receive a pick up but are you happier at catching one or two when you could be catching five or six?

I'm not, so I often tailor my lead systems to suit. Generally, it was semi-fixed arrangements that the carp found easy to deal with – such as lead clips or inline lead presentations. I'm not saying that you should never use a clip or drop off inline because they're the way forward when targeting carp in weed, but on clear, hard lake beds I think you should experiment with a running system or a presentation I call 'The Shokka'.

The idea of the Shokka is that you gain the best of both worlds – a free running rig with ultra-sensitive bite indication, but with the same aspect as a bolt rig. Consequently, your main line should be fished extremely slack with the bobbins laying on the floor. Not only will this sink your end tackle and conceal it on the lake bed, it will also allow sufficient movement. In other words, as the carp sucks in the hook bait it will be able to move several inches before hitting any resistance. Conversely, on a tight line they'd feel resistance immediately and, just like with a lead clip, use that extra weight to discard the hook.

THE SHOKKA RIG

To form the rig, you will need to remove the insert from an inline lead. Take a Safezone Leader of your choice, it's better to match it to the colour of the lake bed, and place a Buffer Bead over the swivel. This cushions the impact of the lead on the cast. Place the inline lead onto the leader so that it is free running and then push a 4mm Rubber Bead over one of the tungsten collars. This acts as the backstop.

01

The components that you will need are, a square pear inline lead, a Safezone ring swivel leader, 4mm beads, shok bead and a Kwik Link.

02

Firstly cut off the ring swivel from the Safezone leader.

03

Replace with a kwik link, this will allow for quick changing of hooklinks.

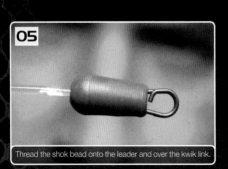

04

Now take the lead and tap out the plastic insert.

05

Thread the shok bead onto the leader and over the kwik link.

06

Now thread your lead onto the leader.

07

With a gate latch needle thread on a 4mm bead.

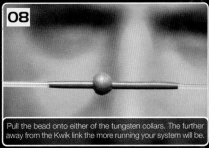

08

Pull the bead onto either of the tungsten collars. The further away from the Kwik link the more running your system will be.

The thinking behind the rig is that a carp may feel safe as it sucks in the bait because there is virtually no resistance as the leader slides through the lead. As a result, it may suck it back even further in the mouth. As it then travels away with the hook bait on a free-running line, bang, it hits the stopper and the weight of the lead. Due to how far back the fish will have sucked in the hook bait the weight of the lead should drive the hook home creating an almighty one toner!

A great lead system that will outwit some of the most pressured fish on the planet.

The other advantage of this presentation is that if the fish picks up the bait, moves off a little and decides all is not right, it doesn't have an anchor point to work against like it would with a semi-fixed lead. Many people now feel that where heavy, semi-fixed leads are overfished carp may be using the heavy lead to help it free the hook without giving indication at the anglers end. This rig overcomes that.

A beautiful 45lb common from a very pressured venue in France. Shokka success!

THE SLIDING LEADCLIP

If you're not a fan of fishing an inline or tend to pinpoint carp in weedier or choddier conditions, you may want to try this version. In some circumstances the lead may plug into the lake bed so an inline wouldn't be the best option. The swivel on the hook link would bury into the bottom and may even leave it sitting at an incorrect angle – this may blow your chances of a pick up completely. However, a lead on a clip has more height to plug into the lake bed, leaving your hooklength laying on top ready to be engulfed by Mr. Carp.

01 All you will need is a Safezone ring swivel leader, Lead Clip, Tail Rubber, Kwik Link and 4mm beads.

02 Cut the ring swivel off the leader.

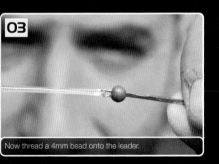

03 Now thread a 4mm bead onto the leader.

04 Place the bead on the 2nd tungsten collar.

05 With a crimping tool carefully just squeeze the front of the Lead Clip, this will help it grip your Kwik Link, this will become clear later.

06 Put your Lead Clip and Tail Rubber onto a stringer needle and thread onto the leader.

07

Now clip on the Kwik Link onto the loop that you cut your ring swivel off.

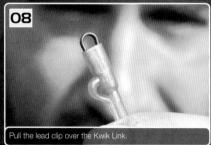

08

Pull the lead clip over the Kwik Link.

The running clip works in exactly the same way as the Shokka and was shown to me by Danny Fairbrass. He and I have managed some magnificent results using this rig. As a fish moves off with the bait it will feel a minor amount of tension as the link is attached inside the clip.

Due to this, the carp will savagely shake its head, releasing the link from the clip back to a free-running system. Then, as it panics the lead will slide up the leader and hit the backstop – one result, nailed!

Running rigs work best in medium range fishing up to 100yrd or so on relatively clear lake beds – gravel, light silt or clay. You don't want any sort of detritus such as weed or lilies to snarl the leader at all because it will prevent the lead from running freely. The bite detection on a running system is far greater than any other lead arrangement out there. Try testing it in a field or garden. Walk the running rig out 60 yards or so attached to your rod and do the same with a semi fixed presentation such as a helicopter or clip. Place them side-by-side and pop each rod onto an alarm both with slack lines.

Turn the alarm up so that you can hear it and then walk back to the leads and pick them both up – one in each hand. Walk backwards, side-to-side, move your arms vertically and you'll notice a big difference. Due to the free movement on the running rig, your alarm and bobbin will respond immediately. However, you may need to move a few feet before the semi-fixed system indicates a bite. Try it for yourself, you'll be amazed.

The finished set-up is neat, tangle free and with the kwik link you can change hooklinks comfortably with either a looped hooklink or link loop.

PASTE BAITS

If I had to pick 3 baits to fish for carp for the rest of my life paste would most definitely be one of them. It really is an underused and misunderstood tactic however it is a devastating one. I have experienced some fantastic session changing experiences and I think it's important that during this carp bait chapter you get an insight into how excellent they can be.

For this chapter I have come to Elphicks day ticket complex in Kent. It has a number of lakes on the site ranging from mixed pools to out and out Carp waters. I have chosen to set up for the short session on Prairie lake which has a fantastic stock of single figure carp up to mid doubles along with a sprinkling of Koi carp and catfish. The plan for today is to show just how devastating paste baits can be and how easy they are to make and use effectively.

For those of you who are new to the game, I will explain briefly about how pastes have evolved in carp fishing. Many moons ago, during the late 1960's and early 70's anglers starting mixing various ingredients to form a paste around the hook. This was different to the normal baits at the time such as black eyed beans, potato's, sweetcorn and bread. For the first time people could incorporate meaty ingredients into their bait and as a result we moved into an era of catfood style pastes which are excellent even to this day. However the main problem with paste was the attention of little fish.

An Elphicks stunner, after a few minutes of casting out with paste.

Keeping them on the hook was a problem as nuisance fish whittled them away and it was this quandary that meant people started to boil paste's to give them a resilient outer skin which we all know now as the 'BOILIE'. The problem with the boiling process is that you can boil some of the attraction out of the paste; however the staying power of the boilie far out weighed the superior attraction of the pastes. Luckily today we have the best of both worlds, fantastic boilies and fantastic fish catching ingredients which means that you can make phenomenal paste baits to compliment your fishing with boilies or other baits no matter what species you're targeting. Paste fishing can really add another element to your angling and acts as one of the best fish pullers I've EVER SEEN! Using them can be fun and you can let your imagination go wild and create something with your own touch of 'uniqueness'!

SLOW BREAKDOWN PASTE

Making your own paste baits couldn't be easier and some of my favourite mixes originate from the base mixes of some of my most successful fish 'slaying' boilies. The Grange boilie from Mainline is now in angling folklore as it was the start of a new generation in boilies. It gave the fish a complete food source in a boilie which satisfied many of their dietary requirements whilst carrying huge pulling power. Therefore as a slow breakdown paste it is also superb.

01 Here is the small selection of items that you need. 1kg Grange CSL base mix, Cornsteep Liquor part 1 and 2 and Pacific Tuna Ade.

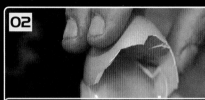

02 When making a slower breakdown paste you should always use eggs, the same as if you're making your own boilies. You can do this easily on the bank. Just crack one egg into a bait tub.

03 Next add 15ml of Mainline Corn steep liquor Part 1. This is what you would normally add to 4 eggs but as I am trying to make something a bit special I'm stepping up the liquid attractor levels.

04 Next add 1ml of CSL Part 2 once again from the Mainline bait stable.

05 Now those last two ingredients alone would be enough to make a great paste however I am going to add a great warm weather flavour called 'Pacific tuna', I am adding 3ml of flavour to one egg. This will make the paste a 'bit special'!

06 Now give the whole lot a quick whisk.

07

It will now be a lovely sticky consistency.

08

Next you need to add the Grange Base mix to the liquid.

09

Now fold the mix together (I sound like Jamie Oliver!) before getting your hands in and moulding the paste.

10

The finished ball will easily last you a couple of sessions, it should be slightly sticky to touch.

QUICK BREAKDOWN PASTE

A slight alternative to the egg based paste is this following little number: It is a method I rate very highly and a bait presentation that can put extra fish on the bank in the most adverse conditions. Because the ingredients breakdown quicker than an egg based paste it has excellent flavour leakage but isn't as resilient as egg based pastes, however if your moulding it around a boilie or a piece of meat it can be amazingly successful.

01 The main binder for the mix is the hookbait Enhancement dip flavoured with Activ-8 which is probably my all time favourite boilie. This liquid is similar in consistency to egg but it is water soluble which means it breaks down much quicker than egg. I add around 30ml into a bait tub.

02 I then add a synthetic flavour for extra pulling power. Spice 'B' is a beautiful cinnamon smelling flavour and compliments the Activ-8 beautifully. It is actually the flavour that I caught my first ever double figure carp on!! I add 2ml of flavour and this will give the paste even more attraction.

03 I then add a cap full of sweetener, this helps to neutralise any bitter taste coming from the flavour, giving the bait a nice sweet note.

04 Start adding some Activ-8 base mix.

05 The mix will be slightly more sloppy with these ingredients.

06 Keep adding the base mix until all the liquid is absorbed.

Time for the hands to get nice and messy.

The mix this time will be far more crumbly compared to the egg based pastes. However it will be pliable enough to mould around a hookbait and give you a level of fish attraction that is unique and very effective.

Making your own paste's can be very fun and developing your own combination of flavours can give you an advantage over other anglers, just make sure you do not go too OTT on the flavour levels and remember to always use a liquid sweetener. These are some of my favourite summer flavours, all smelly and 'fishy'.

Fruit flavours are good all year round but in the winter they are better than 'fishy' smelling ones. Pineapple is probably the best flavour I have ever used in any hookbait during the winter.

GETTING THE BEST OUT OF YOUR PASTE

I like to mould paste around a boilie to give my single hookbaits extra pulling power. It really does make a big difference compared to a boilie on its own. Coupled with an IQ2 hooklink and size IO Wide Gape B you have a combination to take commercial fisheries apart.

01

Mould the paste around a boilie of your choice.

02

Drop the paste ball along with a few different sized pellets into a Korda Funnel web PVA tube.

03

Tie the Funnel web bag off nice and tightly, if your unsure how to do this, then just follow the instructions on the front of the Korda Funnel web tube.

04

Next push through a gated boilie needle.

05

Hook the needle end onto the loop on your hair, you will need a hair of around 1inch in length to squeeze on the 50p sized PVA bag. Now thread the bag on.

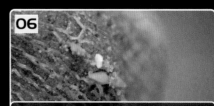

06

Push a boilie stop or Extenda stop through the loop on the hair to secure the bag in position. What you have now is a PVA bag on the hair with the hair running through the centre of your hookbait.

A big irresistible mouthful.

If you're fishing on a lake with a weedy or silty bottom, then try moulding a nice 18mm ball of paste around an 8mm cork ball that has been threaded on the hair. This will give you a critically balanced hookbait which will sit gently on top of any bottom debris or weed.

I like to push a small amount of pellets into the paste which will mean you are adding even more 'punch' to your presentation and whilst varying the breakdown of your hookbait, once again giving you something different to help put more fish on the bank!

Similar to the small pellet tip, I like to dust my paste hookbait in a good groundbait. The new activated Nut mix is perfect as it has a few lumps of different nuts in there to give your hookbait a real edge. As it lands on the bottom the dusting of groundbait will form a haze around your hookbait for added visual attraction.

CONCLUSION

Once the photography was done for this chapter, I managed to wet a line for a short while, and on the very pastes that we made, the action was fast and furious. Even though the fish were enjoying the spring sunshine the paste managed to lure fish down to the bottom and produce instant action and results, with some fabulous Elphicks carp. Paste fishing really has come on leaps and bounds. Match anglers use it very differently to the way I do, however in both disciplines it is a brilliant tactic. With the baits I have covered, you can literally use them on their own, or moulded around any type of hookbait.

Even when you're making your own, there really are no limits as to what you can add to make your own unique paste. As it's a paste you're not sealing the attraction in like harder baits such as boilies. Add things such as tinned tuna in brine, sausage meat, luncheon meat, sweetcorn, liquidised particle etc etc. Let your imagination go wild (within reason!!!), and concoct something 'special'. The ones I have shown you are simple to make and devastatingly effective. Get out there and get on the paste it really can make a difference on so many waters. It's not just limited to carp either, you will bag up on all species with paste, including big barbel, tench, bream and chub. Like any good bait, they catch anything that swims!

I've been lucky to land some huge fish on paste both a home and abroad.

MEAT FEAST

When the cold sets in, certain types of bait find a permanent place in my bait bag. I always look for an edge over other anglers and one such bait that gives me this advantage is meat in its various guises. Its funny how certain baits come in and out of fashion, but like a good 'aftershave' they never lose their effect! It seems like years ago (almost two decades!) since I caught my first specimen carp on 'meat'. in fact it was a humble cube of spam just hair-rigged on and chucked in the pond that did the damage!

I will never forget the effectiveness of meat from those early days of carp fishing and just how many fish a single tin of meat could put on the bank! I won my first ever club match with meat back in the early nineties during the winter and ever since I have experimented heavily with different ways of applying and using it. These days we are spoilt for choice with lots of different options available on the supermarket shelves and also in tackle shops.

Pepperami, luncheon meat, meatballs, frankfurters, chorizo, sausage meat and much more all have a place in fishing. I have caught 100's of specimen fish on all of these baits, so the challenge was set to display and present some tactics to you guys. Former Total coarse fishing editor Gareth Purnell has never seen or landed a Pepperami caught carp, it was my job to catch a few on various tactics and to display a few top tips that will hopefully change his luck with the 'rami'! I am a huge believer in it being a great winter bait, and I wanted to show you a few of the tactics that I employ to have a bumper day using meat! Gerards lake near Peterborough was the venue, for a 'meaty attack', to add to the challenge, it's a venue I've never been to!

FLAVOURING MEAT

01

First chop up a few cubes of spam, and then place them in a small bag.

02

Next add a good squeeze of Predator plus, the 'bloody' liquid soaks into the meat and then lets off and irresistible scent over a period of time. I got this top tip off Bait-tech female supremo Wendy Lythgoe, when international superstars talk I listen! Get on it.

RAMI

My all time favourite meat bait is pepperami, it's almost like it was made for angling rather than eating, even though they are mightily tasty! They are tough which makes them perfect for hair-rigging, they are full of garlic and fat sources which fish adore. More recently they have released chilli versions and fish love chilli, which makes these a truly awesome hookbait. If you haven't used them before then read on and then make sure you have a stick in your bag next time you go angling! You won't be disappointed.

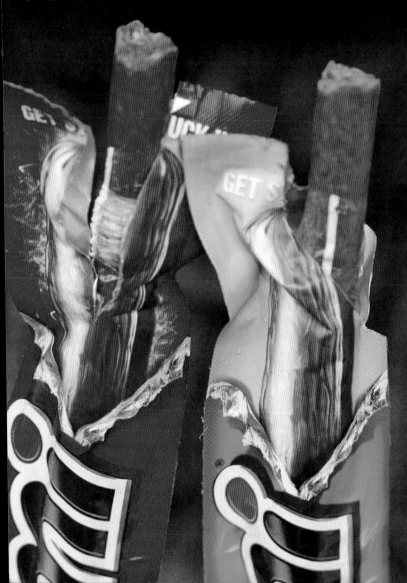

SPAMMING

Back in my day (god I feel old!), there used to be only one type of luncheon meat, these days you can buy it in different forms and flavours. I like the garlic or black pepper versions. Garlic and black pepper are great taste and attraction enhancers which in my eyes make these a much better choice than the plain stuff. Fishing with meat is limited only by your imagination. I will explain more about spices later.

Batchelors meatballs, a truly awesome barbel and carp bait. They are very soft which only makes them suitable for margin work and gentle casts, but boy do fish love em'!

Herta Frankfurters are a bait that I enjoyed one of my best ever Barbel sessions on in Greece some many moons ago! They are not as meaty smelling as some other sausages, however many top specimen anglers favour them for their river assaults. They are much tougher than meatballs and can be cast a lot further due to their durable skin.

SPICE IT UP

One of my greatest meat results came back in the nineties, when the previous night I 'stunk' our family kitchen out frying meat in 'Tumeric'! I learnt a huge lesson that day, when the rod with a 'tumeric' infused piece of meat kept getting sucked up by carp whilst the standard cube out the tin remained untouched. It was an important lesson learnt early in my fishing career. Ever since this emphatically one way experience, I have played around a lot with spicing up my baits with different powdered spices. Tumeric, Chilli Powder, Paprika and Madras curry powder are my top four. The process is very easy to undertake.

01 Firstly chop up a selection of different meats.

02 Next add a table spoon of spice to your hookbaits. Chilli powder is my top choice in the winter!

03 On a low heat now start to fry the powder and the meat together which should gradually infuse the meat with a delightful carp catching aroma! Don't taste it unless you have a very strong resilience to 'hot food'!

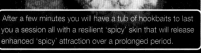

04 After a few minutes you will have a tub of hookbaits to last you a session all with a resilient 'spicy' skin that will release enhanced 'spicy' attraction over a prolonged period.

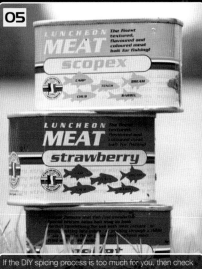

05 If the DIY spicing process is too much for you, then check out some of the flavoured meat by Van Den Eynde. I have used this for years and rate it very highly. Feeding mixed flavours introduces different scents and colours into the swim which can only induce a positive feeding response.

THE ADAPTABLE PVA METHOD MIX

Because a lot of my fishing consists of very short sessions, I don't have enough time to knock up both a method mix and then a separate PVA bag mix. I have experimented a lot in the past and have a combination of ingredients that make both a wonderful and durable method mix, but also a deadly PVA mixture. It doesn't cost a lot and is very easy to do.

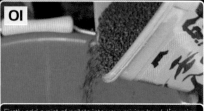

01
Firstly add a pint of pellets into your mixing bowl, I'm using the 3mm Bait-Tech Halibut Pellets which have been superb for a number of anglers.

02
Next add half a pint of Special 'G' groundbait. This is a great binding groundbait and very adaptable so you don't need a huge amount for this mix.

03
Give the whole lot a mix up and then put a kettle full of water on the boil!

04
While you're waiting for the water to boil, sprinkle about two table spoons of chilli powder over your groundbait and pellet combo.

05
Now carefully pour boiling water over the pellets so you give the whole lot a coating, but not so that it's swimming in water. If it's easier, add it bit by bit.

06
Carefully mix the whole lot up, if you have sensitive skin then wear rubber gloves.

07

Now like a cheese grater would, grate half a tin of meat through your groundbait riddle and into your mix. This will compliment the chilli superbly and give the mix a sticky, binding, meaty texture and scent.

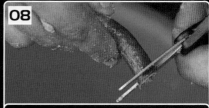

08

Now cut up a stick of pepperami into the mix, so that fish don't get preoccupied on one size of bait, making them difficult to catch.

09

A handful of bait should look like so, a lot of spice and flavour, with a few bigger bits in each handful. Leave for half an hour to absorb all the water and flavour.

IO

Take a handful of bait, mould it around your feeder, before you do the final bind, fold your hooklink into the ball and then add a bit more mix to trap the link into it, leaving it tangle proof and cocked to 'nail' a feeding carp!

A MEATY RIG

What's great about this rig is that with a few Extenda stops at your disposal, you're able to adjust the rig to suit different sized baits. This means you do not have to change the rig every time, just a quick change in Extenda stop means you can use either a larger or smaller bait. Simple.

01

My favourite pattern of hook for the colder months when I'm looking to use a more delicate set-up is the Korda Wide Gape in size 12 Barbed or size 10 Wide Gape B on waters with a barbless only rule like Gerards.

02

Firstly with the aid of the Korda Strippa tool.

03

Strip 4 inches of coating from 12inches of Korda Hybrid hooklink, which has a soft nature to it making it ideal for use on various lakebeds.

04

Then make a small over hand loop at the end of the exposed braid, this will form the loop for your hair rig.

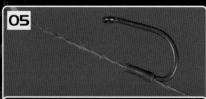

05

Now thread on 3mm of 0.5mm silicon tube on your hooklink, then you need to work this onto your hook point. Thread this on with the point pushing through at the end furthest away from the loop.

06

Position this on the bend of the hook once threaded through and leave yourself about an inch of hair, which should allow you to use different hookbaits.

07

An essential part of effectively using meat is to incorporate an Extenda stop. These are excellent at forming a spine for softer baits so that the hair does not tear through the bait on the cast. Due to the varying lengths of them, you can use them also to extend the length of your hair.

08

Use the small Extenda stop on Pepperami.

09

I use the medium Extenda stop on luncheon meat, this absorbs some of the shock on the cast and allows you to vary the size of your meat by changing the size of Extenda stop where necessary.

10

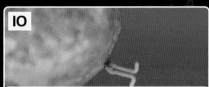

For meatballs, I use the large extenda stop. However even with the Extenda stop I still feel the bait is too soft for casting. A gentle lob at close range is generally all that a soft meatball can take. Tougher versions are available like the Swedish meatball, but I haven't used these before.

Well there we have it, I hope that is quite a comprehensive list of tips for you to employ on your next session. The session today has been a massive success and I would be lying if I said I have fished for longer than two hours! The rest of the anglers have caught very little, whilst I have struggled to keep a rod in the water. That's not showing off, it's just a reflection of how successful the tactics have been today.

After locating fish in the middle of the lake, I have presented a rod on my PVA set-up and also one on the method feeder on the exact set-up and mix which I have covered. The PVA set-up has out-caught the method 2:1, with 6 landed on the PVA and 3 on the method. On reflection I think this signifies how the lake was fishing. With the lack of action around the lake, it was obvious that the easy little mouthful of bait in the Funnel web bag was being attacked far quicker than the method.

However they obviously loved the mix and the pepperami hookbait. I introduced no freebies, and left it completely down to the power of the pellet combo and meaty hookbaits. It truly is a great way of fishing and something that I will be using a lot during the colder months. Ignore these methods at your peril, they're both easy to use and inexpensive making meat an ideal tactical option.

WINNING BALLS

Boilies boilies boilies, for what its worth I don't believe any other bait has had as big an impact as boilies have had on specimen fishing around Europe. Since the days when Mr Wilton et al first boiled their bits of paste to give them a skin to deter the attentions of nuisance fish, anglers have never had it so good. The plan in this chapter is to take you through some of my top tips for boilie fishing but also to relive some of the fantastic successes that I have enjoyed with the best big carp bait of all time.

Now don't get me wrong, I genuinely believe in the pulling power of all manner of baits and these chapters have been showing and will continue to show you a true insight into the benefits of a whole spectrum of baits. However when it comes to targeting big carp then I would very rarely go fishing without boilies.

The whole idea of the boilie was to produce a bait that carried the attraction of some of the fabulous paste concoctions that people conjured up, but be able to withstand the persistent attention of nuisance fish. The more time with your bait in the water meant more carp, and when the boilie was finally coupled with the hair rig back in the 70's, suddenly average anglers where transferred into fish catching machines! Apart from the hair rig, it's hard to recall too many things that have had as bigger influence on the big fish hunt as the humble boilie. However nowadays, anglers targeting all manner of specimens will use boilies. barbel, bream, tench and even big roach love boilies and top anglers targeting these fish will often use boilies to single out larger fish.

Why do fish love them so much? Well things have moved on a lot since the first homemade boilies that graced the boiling pans years ago. The days of basic ingredients such as soya flour and semolina being the bulk make-up of a boilie are long gone. These days a good majority of the baits on the tackle shop shelves and freezers contain enough ingredients to form a very good diet for fish and enough goodness to give them the catalyst for growth and weight gain. In fact fish of all sizes love them and that's what makes them such an amazingly good bait.

A stunning 35lb 10oz Activ-8 caught mirror.

Like us we know when we love something and generally we want more, a good boilie is no different. I have caught large specimen tench, bream and carp on all manner of baits, but thinking back and looking back through captures, the vast majority of my largest specimens have fallen to boilies.

My biggest carp (55lb 15oz foreign, 40lb 10oz UK), my biggest tench (10lb 8oz) and my biggest bream (12lb 10z) have all fallen to boilies and its no coincidence. Don't get me wrong fish of all sizes will eat them, especially small ravenous carp, but a good boilie breeds success with big fish, because the high quality ingredients leaves them wanting more and the more you put in the more they want and the greed factor takes over. In a lot of my magazine and TV work you will see Mainline boilies. A lot of people think that I promote these because I get paid by them or get them free. I won't disagree that by being in the angling industry I'm in the privileged situation of getting tackle and bait free, however what people forget is that we get sponsorship deals thrown at us regularly. However I will only use the best tackle and bait.

The shops are rammed with choice, but hand on heart I have never used a better boilie than a Mainline one. I don't get paid to say that, I use their bait because I want to. Just using 2006-2009 as a yard stick. I first got hold of my first batch of Cell boilies back in 2006, and they have gone from venue to venue and produced magnificent results whilst I've watched other baits fail miserably. This gives you so much confidence in a boilie and the manufacturer, and when Mainline keep on producing these wonder baits, why should I use anything else?

My first 50 at 51lb 2oz caught on Mainline GLM Plum.

THE GRANGE PHENOMENON

The Grange boilie by Mainline marked a new era in boilies, this bait was not your common highly flavoured boilie with a scent and a colour. In fact in colour and smell it doesn't jump out the bag and bite you on the nose like some baits on the shelf, which in this case was a very good thing. But as they say, never judge a book by its cover because this boilie was a ruthless fish hauler! For the first time ever an average additive called corn steep liquor was put into a bait and partnered with ingredients that activated the bait in such away that an irresistible signal was released from the bait that fish could not resist. Not only is it good for the fish, but it was also a highly attractive boilie. Average anglers were turned into bag up gods overnight, and I'm not exaggerating. On difficult lakes the same fish where being caught time and time again on the Grange due to its effectiveness. This was the birthchild of the reactionary bait era and set a new landmark in bait development. From its launch in the early 90's it still remains a phenomenal fish catcher even to this day, testimony indeed to the quality of ingredients and the way that they came to life when immersed in water. Attraction is more than smell, the signal and taste of bait is far more important than the 'label' that a bait has when flavoured, a very important FACT!

THE ACTIV-8

After the Grange came probably the most successful bait of all time. Whenever I fish a new lake I always take the ACTIV-8 especially if I know it has never been used on that lake. This bait has a wonderful marmite esque meaty aroma, but once again it's not a flavour, it is a result of a liquid food that is combined with the powdered ingredients that produces a total food bait for the carp. When immersed in water this bait comes alive and releases an abundance of natural attraction that fish cannot resist and when they taste one, like a Pringle advert the fish can't stop. Amazingly the Activ-8 is a great roach bait in small sizes! I have caught some of my biggest carp using it and I know it will catch me many more in years to come. It truly is an all time classic, that will never fail.

SHELF-LIFES

One of the elements that confuses new comers is the difference between a freezer bait and ready-made shelf life boilie. Now in my opinion a freezer bait is a better all round boilie and far more suited to long term application, however shelf life's will always have a place in angling because they offer people something different. Shelf life boilies rarely contain the top end ingredients that a more expensive freezer bait does, however they are high in attraction and are generally more visible in colour which makes them excellent for those of you with limited time, fishing very short sessions. A small patch of boilies around a hookbait can be a recipe for success and with great flavours available such as Tutti-Fruity, Strawberry, Pineapple, Tigernut and Halibut, the day session angler is spoilt for choice. Fish will eat these for ever and that's why I always carry a bag with me just for a different option. My all time favourite is Pineapple Opals or Plum, give them a go.

FISHMEALS

Away from the reactionary baits that I have covered, another great form of bait is the fishmeal, this is once again a great food source for carp. There are many on the market, but I have recently experimented with a couple from the Baitworks stable and also from Heathrow Bait Services. These are different to birdfood mixes, but contain very instantly attractive ingredients. Look for ones with chilli or Robin Red powders in. These carry a bit of extra punch. If you would like some excellent short session hookbaits then try Heathrow baits Super stench boilies, which are packed with tuna, which by now you should know is one of my all time favourite ingredients!

CUTTING EDGE

Now one of the negatives of boilies due to the constant stream of them entering our lakes is the shape. Almost every boilie you will buy is round. This makes them great for catapulting out, but unfortunately the fish soon wise up to the fact that little round balls equal danger! Yes they love to eat them and eventually they will, however something that I always do to speed up the time between bites is to trim my baits into odd shapes, this takes away the visual outline of a round boilie and makes suspicious carp or other fish a little bit more accommodating when you have limited time. This really does make a huge difference. It turns a 'dangerous' looking bait into a safe looking one. Couple this with a small Korda Funnel web bag of chopped boilies and you have the perfect little trap for cautious carp on any day ticket water around the country.

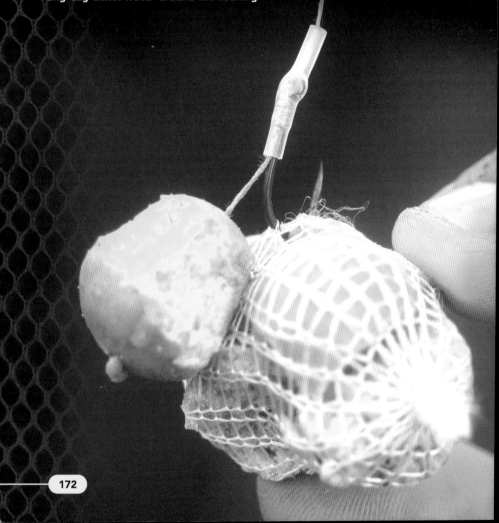

CHOPS

If I was to limit myself to one style of bait for the rest of my life when targeting big bream, tench, barbel and carp, I would commit to using an all time classic combination that has worked wonders for my fishing. I have caught carp ranging from 1lb-50lb on this combination. It is very simple and basically includes a jar of Bait-techs amazing parti-blend and then a chopped boilie of my choice. I then have the option of fishing a small cut down boilie over the top, with a little Korda Funnel web bag. It really is a devastating tactic and one that will continue catching for years to come.

Something that a lot of anglers do wrong is to fish a small PVA bag of pellets with a giant 20mm boilie. This screams danger to the carp! A great short session tactic or when fishing over particle baits is to use a small PVA bag of mixed sized pellets and then present a dumbbell shaped bait over the top, these resemble pellets and won't force the carp to spit them out due to them feeling larger, heavier and a distinctly different shape. Alien objects are often rejected as unwanted objects by fish, therefore a small pellet shaped boilie can often be more acceptable to shy fish than a great big round one. Always carry a tub of dumbbell baits for a quick fix, they have all the same ingredients, but they are a different shape that fish do not associate with danger.

SHAPE UP!

Again on the subject of shape, I have had great success with two halves of a round boilie back to back. This is once again a massive edge that you can be sure other anglers won't be using. It gives you so many options and fish once again will eat it with confidence rather than a degree of caution. All these minor adjustments which only involve a pair of scissors can turn a fruitless session into a successful one, I'm not kidding you!

My final tip for quick success is to utilise bait dips. Again these can provide you with that necessary edge on any given day. They just give your hookbait that little bit more pulling power which can often lure the fish down to the hookbait in amongst your free offerings. Like changing the shape of your bait, these can also make a massive difference to your catch rate. Don't be afraid to experiment, that's half the fun and is only limited by your imagination.

Well there we have it, boilies done. I can't grumble, however I could have easily written 3 times what I have here on these baits. There is so much to tell and so many stories to relive that I could fill the whole book talking about how great boilies are. If you would like more boilie fishing tips then visit my page on www.korda.co.uk

CELL!

THE CELL IS RADICALLY DIFFERENT FROM OTHER CARP BAITS

CELL!

T OFFERS A PROTEIN SOURCE THAT'S EASIER TO DIGEST THAN FISHMEAL OR BIRDFOODS

CELL!

HE CELL HAS DELIVERED UNPRECEDENTED ESULTS, BOTH INSTANTLY AND LONG-TERM.

That's three good reasons to buy, buy, buy THE CELL from Mainline. For more good reasons, this is what Laney had to say... "This thirty-six pound mirror from Suffolk is one of over 35 thirties and host of twenties I caught during the Cell's one and a half year testing period."

"Not only did the Cell turn waters on their ads with regards to catch rates but the fish showed a marked provement in growth rates over this period compared to previous years."

"Once the bait was available on general release, the other anglers who ntinued using it on the waters it had been tested on had outstanding sults, far in excess of what s expected on these ters... Just goes to prove w a good bait will just keep working and working, gardless of how many times e fish are caught on it."

r thousands more good asons to use Mainline its, click www.mainline-baits.com **d find out what you're missing out on.**

Cell is available as a dedicated base mix together with The Cell Activator Additive, reshly frozen boilies in 10, 15 and 18mm sizes, freshly frozen Dumbells, Response Pellets, mbell Hookers, Pop-Ups and Paste. See website for full details.

Dedicated carp baits for dedicated anglers

SURFACE BAITS

Many of you reading this chapter will yet to have ever attempted surface fishing. Maybe you're still yet to catch consistently off the bottom or have little confidence in trying this method. However it's great fun and I should try my best to guide you through a few key tips and principles that any successful surface angler should have in their mental armoury!

I certainly do not profess to be as proficient a surface angler as I think I am on the bottom, and in fact I have been lucky enough to pluck certain elements from far more experienced surface anglers than myself. What I have learnt is that surface fishing is an art-form that anyone with a bit of desire and love of the romance of the sport can adopt and employ. There quite simply is no rocket science to surface fishing, however like fishing on the bottom, good practice breeds good results.

For this particular chapter I am once again at the famous Layer Pit in Colchester, Essex. This lake is rooted in my upbringing and I have been carp fishing on and off here for the past 15 years. Some of my fondest childhood memories floater fishing are on this particular venue and I felt it lent itself perfectly to form the base for this chapter. For those of you who are not familiar with Layer the stock is probably in excess of 2000 carp in some 20 acres, with an average stamp of beautiful lean powerful common carp of 12-15lb. In amongst these are around 200 hundred plus 20lb fish with a handful of 30's and one recently caught 40lb Linear mirror. It is quite simply the most unique venue in the UK, because it offers so much to the club angler, and I genuinely believe that if this wasn't on my doorstep as a youngster I wouldn't have developed many of the skills that I have now today.

On this particular trip, I turned up to the lake early evening to discover that the fish were spawning which wasn't great news but I felt with a bit of hard work we stood a chance as the temperature started to drop after around 8pm. However before then, I was keen on showing the photographer a few of my tips, to help you get out there and catch your own surface caught carp on your next outing.

One of the fun parts of floater fishing, is making your way up the aisle at Tesco's and buying some floating baits. Some of the best floating baits I have ever used have been catfoods from supermarkets. They are generally floating biscuits that come in numerous awesome carp catching flavours such as tuna or chicken. Additionally they're in lots of different shapes and sizes which is also very important, I will explain why later.

One of the all time classic floating baits has been the standard 'Chum mixer'. This is still a regular feature in my baiting approach when floater fishing and I don't think you can beat the original version.

The legendary chum mixer.

Remember to catapult the different sized baits out separately as the small baits will land short and the bigger baits long!

Another great inclusion in your bait bag when floater fishing has to be floating trout pellets. I like to use both a high oil version and a low oil version. This gives off different attraction levels and they are also different shades on the surface, which is another aid to fooling fish when surface fishing. These are very attractive, and carp go crazy on them.

However as I explained, there is a bit more to this little bait description. One of the key things that you must remember, is that fishing on the surface shouldn't be treated too differently to fishing on the bottom. I mix the baits that I have mentioned in equal measures into a bucket. The mixed sizes, smells and shapes are vital in combating the potential of fish getting pre-occupied on one size of bait. When floater fishing, one of the biggest problems I hear about, is anglers not being able to get the fish to take their hookbait. The reason for this, is simple. If you feed one size of bait, and then fish something completely different over the top, then the fish are likely to refuse it. However by mix and matching it, you're making it 20 times harder for the fish to distinguish between a dangerous hookbait or the freebies. This completely mirrors how I fish on the bottom. I like to have different breakdowns, smells, sizes and colours in my groundbait or spod mixes for exactly the same reason. This way fish get pre-occupied in the correct way, they are used to eating different sizes, shapes and smells, therefore when they come round to your hookbait, they throw caution to the wind and then BANG.......YOU'RE IN!!!

I have discovered that this Bait-Tech Tuna and CSL soak is awesome at getting the fish going mental on the surface. When the fishing is really slow on the surface, I always like to add something a bit different to my floating baits to provoke a feeding reaction from the carp, and this liquid certainly has the desired effect.

Now read this point carefully as it's probably the number one GOLDEN rule when floater fishing. GET THEM FEEDING before you cast out. It is rare when fishing on the bottom, to have the luxury of watching your quarry and reacting to their behaviour. Surface fishing is different; you are in the privileged situation of being able to watch the fish react to your baiting. One of the first things I do, when spotting fish on the surface is to catapult some bait near them but not on their heads and observe their reaction. On lakes with a low stock or heavily pressured day ticket lakes, the fish can be more tricky to tease, however on commercial pools or club lakes, the fish will often come up to investigate.

The key here when they start feeding is to keep baiting, but under no circumstances cast a line in amongst them, as very quickly the fish can sense that something is wrong before they have developed enough confidence to make regular mistakes! I like to watch fish hoovering off the surface before I present a bait, almost swimming on the surface with their mouths open, my mate Joe Morgan describes them as Piranhas! They are literally swimming round looking for the next floater! That's the time to get your rig in. Obviously they won't always feed like this, but always strive to get them feeding as confidently as you can before you wet a line, and the final point is, don't CAST right on top of the fish. Try to cast past where the feeding fish are and then draw your hookbait back over the top of them, this stops you from spooking confident fish.

Never ignore little quiet corners that have fish milling around in, I always like to bait a few areas and see where fish respond, sometimes just because fish are not feeding in one spot, doesn't mean there won't be a 'pocket' of feeding fish elsewhere.

Floater fishing set-ups don't need to be complicated at all, some of the best floater anglers in the country, use the simplest of set-ups. Firstly I thread 2 float stops onto my line, followed by my medium sized controller. I then follow this up with 2 small 4mm Korda Safezone beads. Once these are on I tie on a size II Korda ring swivel. I then push on one bead on the barrel of the swivel and have the other one half over the eye. I then slide the float stops up so there is a small gap of about I inch for the controller to move between. I will then add around a 4-6ft hooklink to this ring swivel which is tipped off with one of the various hook presentations that I cover in this chapter.

Presentations do not need to be complicated, but I do like a nice light presentation when a snag free situation allows me. The Korda size 12 Wide Gapes and the 8lb Double Strength line from Drennan are mainstays in my approach.

My good friend Adam Penning who is a sensational surface angler swears by the Enterprise tackle artificial mixer. These have a shot on one side which flips the mixer meaning when you side hook them, the hook faces the sky, meaning the fish never see it, ideal for rig shy fish! This is so simple to tie, just Palomar knot the double strength to the size 12 Wide Gape, then simply side hook your fake bait on. Then just tie around 4-6ft of hook link to your size 11 Korda ring swivel.

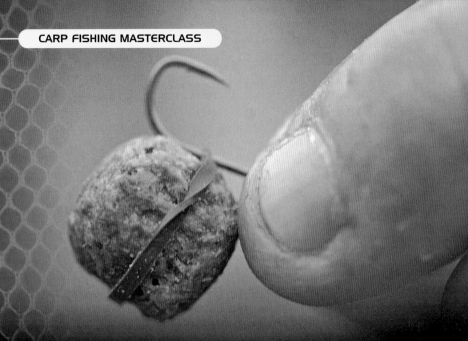

For those of you just starting, then I wouldn't stray too far from a simple bait band set-up. Tie your hook on, add the bait band then simply fit your bait into the band. It isn't the best for pressured fish as I think too much hook is on show and the buoyant bait tight to the hook is too easy to get rid of, however on well stocked venues, this is a nice quick set-up to use. However if you are struggling then try some of the other presentations in this chapter.

  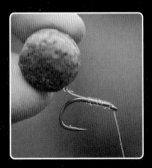

This presentation is ideal middle ground and something I'm sure all of you can tie. Firstly I tie a slip knot at the end of my hooklink, basically a grinner knot. This forms a 'lassoo'. To pull around the bait. With the bait in place, I then tie this to the hook with a knotless knot. This makes life a lot easier than drilling brittle chum mixers for hookbaits. I like to leave a few baits in a bait tub with water to soften, so that the lassoo can bite into it.

A balanced set-up is vital when floater fishing and it also it adds more finesse. Because you're using light hooklinks and small hooks, it's important that you don't then go and ruin that detailed approach with a broom stick rod of 2.75lb TC or more. Of course if I was fishing in snaggy surroundings I would bump all my tackle up, however in most situations, my Tribal Heavy Flood rod is the perfect floater rod. With standard float tip section on, the rod is 1.75lb TC and this provides me with a base to enjoy some fabulous sport, yet has enough back bone to turn mid-sized carp from possible hazards, however I would be happy to use this even when fishing for really big carp. It truly is a joy to play fish with these rods as you feel every lunge and run from a hard fighting fish. So don't just use a broom stick, try to keep the romance in the approach and use a rod that will keep you in touch with that fish, will not jerk a small hook out, or break a light hooklink.

Something that I'm surprised more people don't do, is fish with braided mainline when surface fishing. It can really aid your overall results. Firstly it floats which is vital when floater fishing, as it gets you in contact with your float quicker, so you are able to strike when a fish sucks down your bait. It also casts further which means you can cast smaller more subtle floats, further. I use the Berkley Whiplash braid, it's really fine and adds to the excitement of the fight as braided line has no stretch, so you feel every turn of the fish. However bear this in mind as the only cushion is in your rod tip and hooklink, so don't give them too much pressure. If you use it properly, it will definitely help you convert more chances into fish on the bank.

Sometimes when there is a wind blowing into my face or when fish are too far out to catapult to, I take the risk of spodding a nice surface carpet of bait out. It really works. Just because it's a bit cumbersome doesn't mean that it will spook fish. If you just cast past the fish, feather the cast so the spod lands gently on the surface, you can quite simply let the bait drift onto the fish either with the breeze or surface tow. Even in flat calm conditions, by watching your freebies, you will recognise a small amount of tow on the surface, so feed accordingly, so that your bait drifts onto fish. This gives you the best possible chance of whipping them up, into a 'frenzy'.

In this particular session the fishing has been hard, but I have kept mobile and gone in search of feeding fish. I have been lucky to find a group of fish that look slightly more likely to feed. I spray a few spods past the fish and let the bait drift over them. As time passes a few start showing interest even though spawning is still firmly on their minds.

Time is ticking and the gates at Layer shut at 10pm which means that as 9:30 arrives I'm still panicking somewhat as fish have yet to feed. However on cue, a few start to get a bit more frenzied, I still haven't seen a true chance to present my bait, therefore I wait a few more minutes before 2 or 3 fish are feeding at the same time. They are really having it now, with a gentle trickle of bait over the top, I manage to keep the fish intensely feeding.

I know now that I only have a small 5 minute window to catch carp. It's now or never. My bait lands some 10ft behind the group of feeding fish slurping happily on my bait, I draw my rig back in amongst them. The light is really falling now, It's hard to make out my hookbait, but it doesn't matter as the rod is nearly pulled out of my hand as a fish sucks up my floating bait and I'm away. After a nice battle I'm rewarded with a nice 12lb common that is a wonderful end to a challenging evening of floater fishing. However I know on another evening, the fish would have been far more accommodating and these methods would have worked much faster, but considering I only had the fish feeding for 20 minutes, it doesn't seem bad at all.

Make sure you get out there, and give these tactics a go. It genuinely is a wonderful method that with a bit of patience can be competently tackled by anyone. Remember to feed, feed, feed, feed before you cast, mix the bait size up and vary your rigs if you're struggling. If you follow those steps and these tips then I'm sure a surface capture won't be too far on the horizon for you all.

PELLETS

I think I used my first trout pellet as loose feed during the season of 1993/94. I had been reading the various catch reports in angling weeklies and noticed the amount of big carp getting caught on small hookbaits over a bed of pellets in PVA bags. At the weekend I got my dad to drive me to a bait and feed supplier and promptly spent all my paper round money on a couple of kg's of these oily trout pellets. I was only 13 at the time and promised myself that I would save up to buy a 25kg sack of these pellets. I like many, experienced some fantastic fishing with pellets, and it was from this era that the pellet boom took place. I started to see more and more people using them and since then it has rocketed to being one of the most popular baits on the market in both the carp and coarse market.

Since those early days the range of pellets has rocketed and if you enter a shop you are inundated with different options. I can imagine it must be quite daunting for many of you just starting up? What do you buy? How do you use it? What's it for? How much do you feed? Invariably like all styles of angling there is an art and a way of getting the best from pellets. Of course fish adore them and will go crazy when you feed them, however it's very difficult to get fish to take a hookbait if they are completely pre-occupied on your loose feed of pellets.

The key with everything is quantity, size and feeding patterns. During the remainder of this chapter I will cover a few different tips that are vital when pellet fishing. If you follow them, you won't go far wrong, and you can enjoy instant action like I have on this evening session. Today I have fished a lake that contains a large head of 5-20lb fish, but they are under constant pressure, which makes them a bit more interesting to target. They are also very 'vintage' looking with beautiful golden flanks. It's the perfect place to spend an hours stalking just to show how effective pellet fishing can be if you feed accordingly and use the right rig to kid the fish into making a mistake. I have come armed with an assortment of tackle, lots of different pellets and my 6ft 6" Shimano Tribal travel rod, so I am travelling lovely and light.

THE HALIBUT

One of my favourite pellets is the 'halibut' pellet. I don't know what it is that makes them so much better than some other types of pellet, but the oil levels, and the attraction levels of them is exceptional. I have started to use the Bait-Tech ones as they come in so many different sizes and options. I always carry a couple of bags in the car, just in case I want to go stalking or to add them to a spod mix.

PRE-DRILLED

One useful option that Bait-tech have introduced, is to sell the larger hookbait Halibut pellets, pre-drilled. This means that you don't have to delicately drill them to put them on the hair. The other important thing to remember when fishing a pellet on the hair is that they can turn soft quite quickly. The halibut ones are the ones I would use for longer day trips, however I will always use a Korda Extenda Stop with these soft baits as it stops the hair from tearing through the bait.

On short day trips you can do a lot worse than to just cast out a Funnel web bag of halibut pellets coupled with a nice 12mm one on the hair. When feeding these I would recommend that you always use a small amount of different sizes. This means you have different breakdowns of bait over a longer period and the fish do not get 'conditioned' to feed on just one size of pellet.

TIME BOMBS!

If you're looking to start using pellets for the first time then take a look at the 'Time Bomb' pellets again from Bait-tech. In here you have an array of different pellets in one bucket, which is perfect for the beginner because it stops you from over feeding one size of bait. Additionally you also have the attraction qualities of all those different pellets meaning you're keeping the fish guessing on both size and smell. Another great version of this is the Pellet combo range from Hinders, I have been using their different pellet combo's for years and once again they have a range of wonderful pellets contained in their 'combo buckets'. You will have variations of betaine pellets, trout and halibut pellets and also a few larger ones for hookbaits.

On a recent filming trip in France, I was lucky enough to be at a lake with the beautiful River Marne running behind it. I used the 'Time Bomb' pellets to great effect by taking a number of barbel and chub, on just the contents of the bucket. I would loose feed a handful of pellets and then fish a 'banded' pellet straight onto a size 12 Korda Wide Gape. This is another presentation option worth considering, a small band hooked on, gives you a quick and easy way of changing hookbait.

RESPONSE PELLETS

These are the pellets that I have been using the longest. Mainlines Response pellets are my all time favourites. I have been using them for over 10 years now and I have lost count of the number of fish I have caught fishing over them. Like all baits that they make, they come armed with the highest quality food ingredients making them rise above others. They come in lots of different flavours and smells. I can assure you that strawberry and fish together smell quite strange, however they work very well. Give them a whirl. As I have emphasised already, use different sizes and smells, as this stops fish from getting preoccupied on just a small bait. Mix these with larger options so that the fish can pick and choose what they eat, because I can guarantee, that if you just feed 4mm Respone pellet, you will generate such a pre-occupied response, and it will be hard to entice a bite.

COMMERCIAL FACE-LIFT

One thing that many of you will face when you visit various commercial fisheries, is that you have to use the pellets that the fishery sells. Generally these are low oil pellets, with very little 'punchy' attraction for the fish. One addition that I have mentioned a hundred times in my writing is just how good 'Tuna' is. I genuinely believe that you can add Tuna to a bad bait, put it in a funnel web bag and suddenly it will be a good one! Next time you go to a commercial fishery with such rules, then remember to add the sacred 'yellow fin'. You will then be fishing bait wise a lot more effectively than the guy who is using the pellets straight out the bag.

OI
All you need is tuna in brine and half a pint of standard pellets.

O2
Now add the tin of tuna to the pellets, juice 'n' all.

O3
Prepare to mash 'n' mix!

O4
Simple, but deadly effective!

EXPANDER PELLETS

The soft expander pellet is something that I have started to use more. They are excellent in a 'spod mix' because they create a lovely scent and lure of attraction with very little food source actually there. They are dripping with water soluble attraction rather than oils which makes them excellent for use all year round. You can also buy matching hookbait pellets to complement your loose feed. This is a type of pellet that you can use if you're just float fishing for carp. You have lots of different flavours available in the Mainline range, so check them out.

If you only have light tackle and want to cast a PVA bag of pellets a long way then the expander pellets are excellent once again. Because they squeeze down so small, you can get a lot into a very small bag by pressing it gently as you tie the Funnel web bag off. The other added advantage when doing this is that bag will be dripping with goodness, and when it bursts on the bottom and expands, that large quantity of squeezed down pellet will be lying all around your hookbait.

As explained you can get matching expander hookbaits to match the smaller loose feed option. I like to hair rig two on a hair and then finish it off with a small Extenda Stop just to cushion the hair from pulling through the pellet. For anglers using much smaller tackle then just one side hooked onto a size 14 or 16 will be adequate for the float angler.

On longer sessions I like to experiment with Enterprise tackles 'artificial' pellets. These are great when fishing over a longer period or when fishing a lake with a large head of nuisance fish that could 'whittle' down a normal pellet hookbait. They do various sizes and options, so check them out. I always carry them, as they can be very useful. Again just simply presented on a hair on a size 12 Wide Gape and 10lb IQ Soft, you have a wonderful subtle presentation to compliment a Funnel web bag of pellets.

Something that has been a pattern through all of these chapters is matching your hookbait to the freebies. I'm not a big fan of using a large round boilie over a small pile of 3-6mm pellets. I always feel more confident when fishing with a dumbbell shaped bait. These can be shaved down or cut in half and come very close to behaving like a pellet. Obviously being a dumbbell shaped boilie they are able to withstand the attention of nuisance fish for a lot longer and will stay on the hair over-night for those 'keener' long session anglers!

LITTLE 'N' OFTEN

The key once you have fish feeding is to feed little and often and to feed with larger items. Once I have fish feeding in the swim like tonight, I will literally just introduce large 8mm pellets so that the freebies match my hookbait, which increases the chance of a bite. If you kept feeding large handfuls of 3mm pellets, then you will just sit frustrated behind a swim full of fish, with little chance of a quick bite.

I could have carried on for a lot longer going into more detail. However pellet fishing isn't complicated. Just ensure you use a good quality bait, present it as I have covered and feed sensibly. Fish love em', and as long as you keep a trickle going in, you will always kid fish into making a mistake. This session has been interesting. I had just shy of an hour to get a few bites, and I managed to catch four beautiful fish in a very short space of time. That is how good pellet fishing can be with one rod, if you get it right, even on a 'tricky' venue.

THE MAGIC GRAIN

Sweetcorn was probably the 2nd bait I ever used to go fishing with after the famous 'loaf'! There isn't a fish that swims that won't eat it. It truly is, a 'legendary' bait in angling terms and continues to produce magical results even to this day with no sign of relenting. For any angler fishing regularly for bream, tench or carp, sweetcorn will and should be a regular fixture in your bait armoury.

A SINGLE GRAIN

Historic angling books such as the 'Carp Strikes Back' brought home to me just how awesome 'corn' can be as a carp bait and so many significant captures have succumbed to the power of sweetcorn. You only have to taste corn, to realise how irresistible that sweet kernel taste is. I always taste baits that I use and sweetcorn has such a beautiful smooth, flavoursome and consistent taste, that it's no surprise that fish have been munching on it for decades.

In modern times we are once again spoilt with the range of corn and maize that is available to us. Long gone are the days when all that one could get was a tin of 'green giant'! There are so many wonderful ways to fish with corn and maize and in this chapter I am going to take you through a number of simple tips that can 'jazz-up' the sacred corn and give it an edge over the standard yellow grain. This is just tip of the ice-berg stuff because there is no end to the ways you can apply it to your fishing, but I promise if you take just a few of these ideas to the bank-side you won't go home with a dry net!

Fishing with a single grain of standard sweetcorn can be difficult over long periods of time because it will not withstand long casts or the persistent attention of nuisance fish, however by using a single grain of 'plastic' corn you are able to present this over a small handful of standard corn and be rest assured that a hookbait remains on your hook until a specimen fish comes along and gulps it up! Additionally coupled with a small size 10 Korda Wide Gape hook, you have a beautiful critically balanced presentation that will behave similarly to the sweetcorn 'freebies' in the swim.

PVA FRIENDLY

Sweetcorn out the tin is obviously going to be damp and unsuitable for PVA bag use. By dusting the corn in a favoured Activated Nut groundbait by Mainline, you are essentially taking the surface damp off the corn, giving you just enough time to present it beautifully in a Korda Funnel web bag.

This is an ideal tactic for those of you who are looking for a quick bite on a short session, this is a scenario that I often find myself in. By simply hooking on the Funnel web bag of corn, coupled with the single grain of plastic corn, you are left with a beautiful presentation, that when cast to showing fish will more often than not result in fish on the bank! It is such a delicate presentation, and one that not many anglers go to the effort of using. Apply it to your next session and you won't be disappointed.

IN THE METHOD

Don't just limit yourself to one colour or flavour. A number of companies do a variety of flavoured and coloured corn. These are some of my favourites and on waters where corn has been heavily used in its standard form, just mixing it up a bit can produce unexpected results. Varying colours and smell in any bait on any given day can be just the tweak that your fishing needs to turn a slow day into a decent one. I have never been one for draining and throwing away the 'juice' from a tin of sweetcorn, and wherever possible I will always try to use it, as a source of liquid to dampen off a groundbait mix, especially when I'm preparing to use the groundbait as a stick mix or method ball.

Corn and the method as a partnership can be deadly. I love making a light fluffy method mix, soaked in sweetcorn juice, with only a small handful of golden grains added to the mix, so that when I hold a handful only a couple of grains are visible in my loose-feed. As result when the groundbait crumbles around the feeder, I am left with a 'fine' food signal but only a limited number of edible food options for the carp which invariably means they will have to feed on my light and subtle double corn hookbait. The mini bait-up method feeder and the corn method mix is an excellent summer tactic, especially if the venue that you're fishing contains any weed or debris on the bottom.

01

The Van den Eynde range of flavoured corn gives a great alternative to the standard green giant!

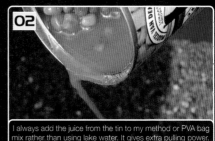
02

I always add the juice from the tin to my method or PVA bag mix rather than using lake water. It gives extra pulling power.

03

To 2 kilo's of method mix I only add a few handfuls of corn, I like my hookbait to be the only real edible hookbait on the method feeder!

04

With a simple helicopter set-up on the feeder I'm ready to lock and load.

SPOD MIX-TASTIC

Corn is one of the most attractive spod mix ingredients that I have ever used. Coupled with a good lashing of hemp, mixed particles and pellets, you are able to produce a wonderful spod soup that is just perfect for 'whipping' the fish up into a feeding frenzy. This style of angling is particularly useful if you're trying to establish an area over a longer session. Maybe you're fishing some longer day sessions or even preparing to do your first night session? If so, I strongly recommend that you add the mixed particle approach to your fishing. It will allow you the opportunity to get fish feeding confidently in your swim over a prolonged period of time. I also really like using this method when I am in marginal fishing situations. With the 'hand of god' or bait spoon as it's more commonly known, I am able to drop my bait and rig tight under marginal bushes and features, which is a wonderful place to present this 'sloppy' corn spod mix.

AMAIZING

I haven't mentioned a lot about maize as a bait up till now, but rightly or wrongly I have always classified it as a member of the sweetcorn family and similarly to corn, fish love it. In fact on many waters around Europe, carp are reared and fed over the close season period with dried maize crumb, now I have always been slightly sceptical regarding the nutritional value of maize, as I'm a strong believer that particles run through fish similarly to a Curry through man, however ironically they are loved just as much as mankind loves a curry! Maize is an option that I often use on venues where the abundance of nuisance fish is just too much, and where even heavy loose feeding with normal corn, stands little chance of withstanding the frenzied feeding of our silver foe. In such instances I will use maize or fake maize on the hook and feed with maize which is much harder and tougher in nature than sweetcorn and slightly larger in size. As a result your chances of lasting the course until a carp or big tench comes along are heightened. If you haven't used maize before then I suggest you investigate it.

When fishing light baits such as corn, it is vital that you get your hookbait to behave as naturally as possible. If the fishing situation allows, I will always try to use a light hooklink such as the 10lb IQ2 which means that I can present my corn hookbaits in such a manner that a pressured fish will not be too cautious in approaching the rig. Simple changes in hooklink really can make a difference to your results, so wherever possible try and use a hooklink like the IQ2 fluorocarbon, which is both low in visibility but also allows the bait to behave naturally.

Critically balanced Maize is a wonderful method over beds of bait or when coupled with a PVA funnel web stick. I like to balance off a single grain of maize with a single grain of plastic pop-up corn. If the set-up is too buoyant, I will snip tiny bits off the edge until the set-up just sinks under the weight of the hook.

On many big carp waters that I have fished, a single grain of maize over a bed of mixed particle is a wonderful approach. A few spods of mixed particle, with a single grain of maize over the top is a deadly presentation. Fish can often get pre-occupied on small seed baits, therefore a bait that is very similar to the loose feed will give you a much bigger advantage than the angler that chooses to fish a larger bait such as a boilie straight over the top.

Throughout this chapter I have spoken about delicate corn set-ups, or single grains of maize. However there have been many occasions when I have used a hair rig with either 3-5 grains of corn/maize on the rig, and this mouthful can be just what the fish doctor ordered for the greedy ones.

SUPERCATCHIN FISHINMAGIC EXTRACLEVER GROUNDBAIT

A groundbait unlike any other! A totally new concept that attracts fish and holds 'em without filling them up. The latest groundbait technology, with a little magic...
MOJO from **Bait-Tech** - CAST THE SPELL.

SEAFOOD PLATTER

It's very rare these days to go on a session and actually learn something new for yourself as the angler presenting the ideas and details. On this particular session my mind was blown away by what I saw and invariably what I learnt. As a part of the carp baits chapters, I was keen to focus one solely on tin and supermarket shelf fish stuff! Hopefully by now, you will be aware of how highly I rate tuna, and in almost every article that I have written in the last few years, I have used it in groundbaits and PVA bag mixes.

Over the past few years or so, I have spent a lot of time talking to Danny Fairbrass, who spends a lot of time playing around with different tinned fish for his stick mixes and has been a real catalyst of ideas for myself and this chapter itself. Certainly during our last Underwater filming shoot we started to play around with a number of different fishy things, but we also held back on a few because we where slightly fearful that we might mess the swim up! This is why I was so excited about this particular session because it was a unique opportunity to see first hand the carp's response to different permutations and bait options. I already know how deadly tuna and sardines are, and I won't go fishing without them, but I've not got as much experience with the other baits.

However to do this properly I needed to do it on a well suited venue. After a chat with good friends Tom Dove and Adam Penning, I gave Mike Barnes a call at Cemex and booked the magnificent Blue Pool lake situated near Reading. The Blue Pool is a gin clear lake with wonderful deep margins and incidentally was the venue where we filmed Part 3 & 4 of the Korda Underwater DVD series. The carp in here have seen a few tricks and won't give themselves up to any old tripe. Therefore with 'evian' like water clarity and an armoury of bait I'm ready to find out once and for all what works and what doesn't. The stock is also phenomenal, with a large head of doubles and 20's with a sprinkling of 30's. It's a venue that has a true stock of stunning jet black English carp.

My initial plan is to bait a few different marginal spots with a lovely mixture of fish and particle, a deadly combination that I have been using for a long time now. Additionally I have a few different larger food items as hookbaits, and I'm excited to see what gets the best response. Over the following pages you will find out how to present them in the stalking approach that I'm going to employ and also a few different applications of fish baits.

SHHHH FISH FOOD!

It really is unbelievable just how little this whole lot costs and the reaction it generates from the carp. These are just my choices for today, but next time you're in the supermarket unearth and test some of the tinned morsels for yourself.

01

I have come armed with a variety of real goodies. Mackerel, sardines, tuna, prawns, mussels, squid, salmon et al!

02

I'm a great believer in adding fish to my bulk feed. So I'm going to show you exactly what I'm feeding with on this session. The Bait Tech Parti-mix is the first thing to go into the bucket, I rate this wonderful aniseed aroma as an all time classic.

03

This tub of goodness alone is enough to build a bumper bag of fish up on. It is crammed full of hemp, tares, maples, maize and smaller seeds, all baits that carp adore.

04

Next add some of this wonderful Chilli hemp. Carp love spicy things and I have been adding chilli to my hemp for years with devastating results. It's a must stay ingredient in any of my bait these days.

05

Now add some 4mm Halibut pellets. These will soak in all the juices from the particle and fish. They will then pump the smell out over a prolonged period of time until the pellet turns into mush.

06

Now for the fish, firstly add a whole tin of Tuna in brine. carp go mad for this stuff, it truly is a magic wand of a bait additive!

07

Give it a good 'flaking' and mix it all into the mix.

08

Now for the sardines in 'chilli Oil'. Put the whole tin in and break the sardines up. They have whole chilli's in the tin, so make sure you add them too.

09

Mash the whole lot up. It should start taking shape now.

10

Now add a handful of mussels from your seafood selection. Mussels have been an integral part of carp fishing for years now.

11

I have also picked out a handful of calamari rings to add into the spod mix. Squid once again is a flavour and bait ingredient that has caught thousands of carp for years now.

13

The finished mix looks irresistible. Now I'll go and spoon it into a few different marginal spots.

12

The sacred prawn, I have to admit that when I first took these out of the seafood selection, they seemed so juicy and meaty that I just couldn't wait to put them on.

I crept up on a few spots that I fancied. One perfect spot was at the end of a fallen oak, that Adam Penning had told me about in swim II. It had a lovely 7ft of depth straight below it and looked like an aquarium. It wasn't long before the carp got on the bait, proving already that the lure of the fish was too much.

I have been using sardines for a couple of seasons now. However I was keen to see the response of the fish to some other variations of it. I already use the chilli version, but I was keen to find out how the one in tomato sauce fairs. Sardine is a lovely oily fish with lots of flavour. Steve Ringer told me that he has been using it in groundbait for years, so if he recommends it then it must be good! The reason I was interested in the tomato juice is that great carp angling legend Rod Hutchinson used to cook black eye beans in tomato soup, and used to rave on about it, so it was worth a go.

Salmon has been the most recent riser in my bait armoury. Danny Fairbrass was playing around with it, and having good results. As a result I wanted to compare it directly with my tuna stick mix. I always use a tinned fish in my stick mix and the tinned salmon has a lovely pungent smell that just screams carp.

FLUOROCARBON FLOAT RIG

For this session I'm going for a simple stalking approach. I have baited 5 marginal areas which now have fish visiting them regularly. The one problem is they all have different depths so. I'm going to approach it with a simple sliding float approach.

01

You will need a pack of size 12 Korda Wide Gapes. A small Drennan loafer float. Some light braid for your hair material. 10lb Korda IQ Soft and a packet of small Extenda stops.

02

Here I am using a back to back grinner knot to join my braided Whiplash mainline to my IQ Soft leader. I am going to add 12 metres as this will give me a nice almost invisible fluorocarbon leader.

03

Next fix on your loafer float with the aid of 2 float bands top and bottom. This will allow me to fix my float to new depths in different swims. The float will then be fished over depth with no shot on the line whatsoever.

04

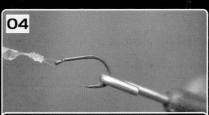

Now tie on your size 12 Wide Gape with a grinner knot to the end of the IQ Soft material. A bare hook is enough if you want to just fish calamari rings as bait.

05

Next cut your calamari into two slivers.

06

All you have to do then is hook the two bits on and you have a lovely super attractive hookbait which is light and should flutter through the water beautifully.

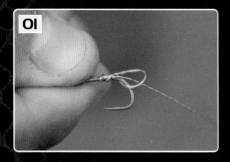

SUPPLE HAIR

For presenting the mussels and prawns as hookbait, I'm going to add a nice supple hair to the hook.

First whip on a length of braid to the hook. Use the shank as the base of the knot. Make a loop and then whip the braid through the loop 4 times then pull it tight.

In effect it's a grinner knot. Cut the tag end facing away from the point off and then tie a loop at the end of an inch of braid which is your hair.

Push a gate latch needle through the darker end of the mussel and then pull onto the hair.

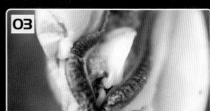

Next put an extenda stop on which will cushion the hair from tearing through the soft skin of the mussel leaving you with a wonderful meaty mouthful.

The prawn on the other hand is quite a tough and meaty bait. Cut one in half. Using the fat half as your hookbait, the bit before the head!

Push through a gate latch needle.

Thread onto the hair then add a small Extenda Stop.

What carp in their right minds could refuse this little lot. It looks awesome, I can't wait to get out there and use it!! It just looks like its going to catch carp, a simple yet effective set-up. Note how I have moved the whipped on hair to the bend of the hook. This makes for better hooking efficiency.

I suppose you're wondering how the session went now that you've seen all the technical shots and action shots? Well as I said at the beginning of this chapter, what unfolded over the next 6 hours or so was mind blowing. The fish really did love the fishy goodies and I was able to distinguish between what was good and what was exceptional. I will explain.

Here's how the session went. As mentioned, I had baited a number of marginal spots, and left them alone while we took the technical pictures for this chapter. Once this was done, I started having a creep around a few of the spots I had baited. I didn't need to travel far as the first spot I visited had clouded up pretty dramatically. I was armed with my hair rigged prawn. I estimated the depth at around 5ft on this spot, so I set the float at 6ft and set about lowering it within the clouds of bait that was being lifted by feeding fish. I watched my prawn flutter through the layers until it were about 2ft from the bottom, then bang! It just vanished and I struck! I was met with solid resistance and a great scrap ensued. These Blue Pool fish really do fight and I could see every twist and turn in the gin clear water. I was in awe as I watch this stunning carp trying to outwit my Tribal Heavy Flood rod, but it took every lunge wonderfully and after some 10 minutes a glorious 18lb linear carp was in the net. First cast with the prawn and bingo! Surely it was just a freak occurrence that the carp took the bait on the drop?

I duly returned the fish and re-baited the spot with the plan to return later. My next cast saw me visit the fallen oak that Adam had told me about in swim II. I peered over the shrubbery at the end of the oak and could see that every drop of bait had been taken. After doing my best scarecrow impression for the next 5 minutes I spotted at least 10 different big carp float over the spot, wanting more food. I dropped a bit more food in and waited. The water here was much clearer than the other swim and I watched fish instantly drop on the spot. It was time to get my prawn in! This swim was much deeper, my prawn was once again fluttering through the water, when a carp literally shot up from the bottom more like a pike to take the hookbait! It was an unbelievable sight to behold.

Obviously the attraction of the prawn coupled with the slow descent of the bait, made this hookbait irresistible to the carp! This was pretty conclusive. A 25lb mirror was the result and another amazing Blue Pool carp. Next I visited yet another hole in the bushes, and proceeded to have the prawn taken on the drop once again! I'm sure the bait descending gently through the water is a 'safe' looking option for the carp, but at the same time, watching these fish chomp the

prawns on the bottom, it was pretty obvious that they loved what they were eating. I couldn't believe what I was seeing. As the session progressed things just got better. In the end I managed to get my prawn to the bottom over feeding carp twice! Other than that the bait was taken on the drop. However each time it did make the bottom, it was sucked up instantly! I just could not believe how well this bait performed. I picked up a nice 20lber on the squid rings, but nothing on the mussel. However to be fair these fish were eating the mussels as loose feed but I never put them in front of real frenzied feeders. Additionally being a heavier bait to the prawns they fell through the water much quicker which meant it was unlikely that they would be taken on the drop.

I could go on for hours explaining what was good and what was exceptional. However I have run out of space. To summarise emphatically, there is nothing I wouldn't use from what I covered in this chapter. The salmon stick mix was amazing and carp tore the bottom up for it. Additionally the sardines in tomato sauce once again received an excited response from the carp. I baited spots with just pellets and none of them received the feeding frenzy that the spots baited with the fish did. Having seen the response to prawns, I don't think I could go fishing without them now. I will gladly fish with it as a hookbait and will be using it a lot more. I caught 7 stunning carp in just a few hours fishing. What I know now is that tinned and fresh fish should be a part of every specimen anglers armoury, it's not just for pike you know! All hail the power of the prawn!

MAGGOT MAGIC

What can you write about the 'maggot' that hasn't already been written before? Well I suppose for the thousands that keep coming into the sport every year, the maggot is seen as a bait that just catches small fish with the chance of picking up bonus fish along the way. In fact that's exactly what I used to think when I first started fishing. If you wanted to catch carp, tench and bream then you needed to fish corn or meat, how wrong I was. My greatest lesson of all was fortunately still in my early angling days at the ripe old age of 13. I was fishing my local pits for 'wild carp' on a bitterly cold winter day!

The fishing was slow for everyone apart from one angler who was obviously using some secret boilie and catching carp after carp. Being the inquisitive type I felt I should get myself round to his part of the lake and have a sniff of these boilies! Much to my surprise as I entered his swim, there wasn't a round ball in sight, maybe he's hiding them because they're so good I thought, at which point his 'quivertip' pulled round and he was into another hard fighting wild carp. After a good five minute scrap, the fish neared the net and with a plastic maggot feeder swinging above its head, things started to slowly fall into place.

It was quite unbelievable really as this was my first insight into how devastating maggots can be for catching carp, especially in the colder months when other baits have slowed down. I continued to pick the mentioned anglers brains and determine exactly how he was using the sacred maggot. Fortunately that early insight into fishing with maggots for carp never blinkered my thinking and even to this day I always consider them as an approach on any venue that I visit.

There isn't a fish that swims that would swim past a maggot, however when used in quantity nuisance fish tend to pale into insignificance and the carp soon get on the feed. In the last few years maggots have seen a bit of a resurgence on the carp scene, mainly through the writing and catches of the great Rob Maylin who has been using a certain 'rig' to great success (more on this later), It was so simple that you just thought you were bound to hook nuisance fish, but what it really did was catch ridiculous amounts of carp!! It seemed like the more maggots you put in the better your results got. Even more recently with the birth of the Korda 'Maggot Klip' it has meant that every angler can now easily present big bunches of maggots ready to fool big carp.

In this particular chapter I am concentrating on how to get the best out of using 'live' maggots, if I had infinite number of pages to cover then I could discuss flavouring and spicing maggots, plus how to kill them on the bank and then use them. However if I had a gun held to my head, I would always use live maggots. In my eyes they are more attractive visually to carp alive and this alone gives them an added advantage! They dig themselves into silt and bottom detritus which means the aggressive nature of carp has them hunting and digging into the bottom! This preoccupation means your rig bares into insignificance as the carp generally hang themselves because they are feeding so hard. However presentation is important so I have covered a number of rig and baiting options that will almost certainly have you catching from the off on maggots.

THE MAG-ALIGNER

This set-up has literally torn waters apart over the past few years. Rob Maylin has caught hundreds of fish on it. The set-up once again is simple to do, and the method can keep you busy even on those really cold winter days.

01

Firstly tie the hook on with a simple knotless knot like so.

02

Cut the tag off which would normally be your hair rig.

03

Using a sharp braid baiting needle pierce the mag aligner grub like so.

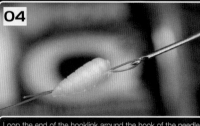

04

Loop the end of the hooklink around the hook of the needle and thread the grub onto the IQ2.

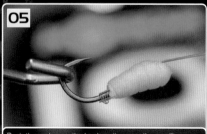

05

Push the grub over the hook so it covers the eye like so.

06

Now hook on two sinking fake maggots like so. Your hooklink is complete.

Take a Safezone ring swivel leader.

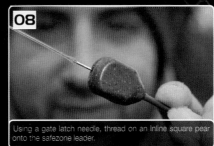

Using a gate latch needle, thread on an Inline square pear onto the safezone leader.

Pull the ring swivel into the plastic insert inside the lead.

Now slide on a size 8 ring swivel, put the ring on the leader rather than the swivel eye.

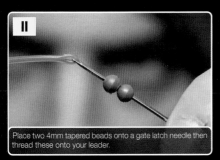

Place two 4mm tapered beads onto a gate latch needle then thread these onto your leader.

The set-up is neat and streamlined.

The important part with a roving approach is a big funnel web bag of maggots.

Once you've tied the bag, leave a long tag end and use this to tie the PVA bag to the ring swivel on the lead. Tangle proof and very attractive.

THE MAGGOT KLIP RIG

When Korda launched the maggot klip, the world went maggot fishing mad! It's amazingly easy to use, no need for needles or floss, just open the klip up and thread the little blighters on! I love the small klip, but I know some people have caught with the large one and a very large ball of maggots! A great specimen hunting item of tackle.

01

The Maggot Klip comes in 4 sizes, X small, small, medium and large. These will cover almost all fishing situations.

02

At the end of the hooklink material of your choice tie on a Maggot Klip.

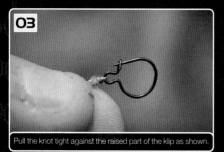

03

Pull the knot tight against the raised part of the klip as shown.

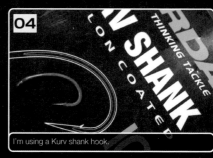

04

I'm using a Kurv shank hook.

05

Tie the hooklink on knotless knot style.

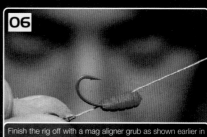

06

Finish the rig off with a mag aligner grub as shown earlier in this chapter.

Open the klip up and thread on your maggots, go for mixed colours.

Have a look at that little mouthful, irresistible!

Well Stanford le Hope has fished slow today with the biting cold easterly wind that has been blowing. We have fished for a couple of hours and the maggots have once again delivered even in the grimmest of conditions. The small spodded area of maggots started to produce the bites and I'm sure if the conditions were slightly warmer I would have probably caught 15 fish in a couple of hours rather than 5! Maggots really can produce the goods when all else fails. Even on lakes with a lot of silver fish, I would still really recommend that you use them in your loose-feed but then try a 'larger' bait on your hair.

Carp absolutely adore maggots and a mix with them in is better than one without them. I do prefer a fresh clean live maggot, but I know friends of mine such as Adam Penning who freeze their maggots in the winter and use them flavoured with liquid carp foods! Like many of the baits in this book, the usage is only limited by your imagination. The Funnel web tactic of casting to any signs of fish can be devastating. I tend to take a gallon for a day session in the winter and my results have benefited as a result. If you follow the tactics in this chapter and find the fish, you will have some bumper days to look forward to.

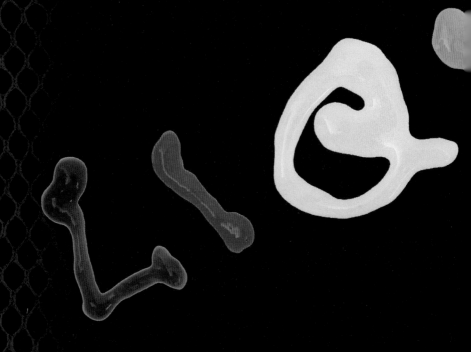

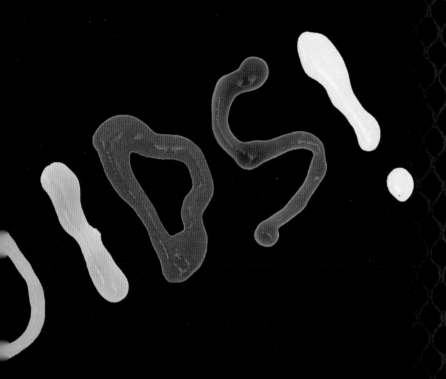

LIQUID SUCCESS

For this chapter I have visited Cemex's Chigborough lake near Maldon in Essex. On a cold December morning it is easy to see why this is going to be one of the top venues in the country. It has lots of bays, Islands and features, which will suit an angler who wants to float fish to one who wants to bivvy up and make a weekend of it. One of the negatives of a beautiful lake like this with so many features, nooks and crannies is that the carp could be held up anywhere in winter! However I have come down at first light to see if I can spot any signs of fish and have been lucky enough to spot a little bit of bubbling in-front of a point which is flanked by two long cigar shaped bays, which will give me stalking options later in the day. The topic for this chapter is to show you how to get the best from the many liquid foods and attractors that are available on the tackle shop shelves.

There are absolutely hundreds these days, but some are better than others, so hopefully this article will help point you in the right direction with regards to where you should spend your hard-earned cash. Also many anglers I see on the banks just do not use liquid foods in their armoury, and I can assure you, when the going gets tough you're missing out on fish. I think one of the biggest reasons they are not used heavily is that many anglers don't know how to get the best from them, so that it puts extra fish on the bank. I have endured some really slow days in the past, both on sweltering hot summer days and freezing cold winter sessions where you have resigned yourself to going home fishless, but a little play with some liquid attractors to substitute bulk food has resulted in instant action. Using them isn't rocket science and over the next few pages you will see some very simple ways of exploiting their effectiveness. There are so many uses for them, that there really is no end to the list of options with them.

DUNKING BAG

This is such a simple thing to do that I'm shocked I don't see more people doing it. With a bottle of dip and a PVA bag, you really can make things happen.

01

Firstly pour a pinch of damp Blitz groundbait into your Korda Funnel web system

02

Then tie the bag off nice and tight like shown. The bag should be the size of a pound coin. This is the perfect size for instant action in the winter. Remember with PVA you're not trying to feed them, you're trying to catch them.

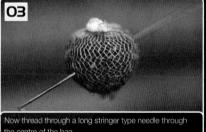

03

Now thread through a long stringer type needle through the centre of the bag.

04

Next comes the good bit, simply dunk the small PVA bag into the bottle of Mainlines hookbait enhancement system, don't worry the liquids I am covering this chapter do not melt PVA, and they are not oil based which makes them perfectly water soluble even in the most arctic of conditions.

Finished and now steeped in attraction. Beautiful!

LIQUID CLOUD

Cold weather often brings with it clear water. This liquid cloud method is a sweet and sour way of producing a lot of smell and attraction without too much substance to fill the fish up with. It can really lure fish in.

01 Take a small bucket and fill it with lake water.

02 Now add a few handfuls of Blitz groundbait to the water and stir it in. This is not a lot of food it just adds to the attraction and cloud factor.

03 Once you have stirred the small amount of groundbait with the water, squirt in some of the Mainline Coconut milk particle and pellet syrup, this stuff tastes gorgeous!

04 Now add around 30ml of Hinders Pineapple or Tiger slime, this stuff is good enough to drink and something that I have used for years. It really is excellent. Give the whole lot a stir and you should be left with a lovely milky coloured liquid.

05 Take one of the Mini Korda Skyliner spods and with the use of electrical tape or this camo tape, cover the holes up to the flights on the body of the spod.

06 Now scoop some of this irresistible cloudy liquid into the spod and then simply cast to the area that your want to fish, be it tight to some marginal bushes, reeds or an area of open water.

The result, an awesome cloud that
will tantalise carp into feeding.

PVA FRIENDLY SWEETCORN

One of the deadliest winter baits is sweetcorn, and I have lost count of the number of fish that it puts on the bank each year. However in its natural form, it will just melt PVA because it inherently carries water. Do not fear there is a very simple way of making this even more effective and PVA friendly.

01

Crack a tin of corn open into the bottom of a bait tub.

02

Now add around 20ml of Pineapple slime to the corn, just enough to coat every grain of corn. The Pineapple slime doesn't melt PVA so by coating the corn in it, it will stop the corn melting the PVA.

03

Give the whole lot a stir.

04

While you're leaving the corn soaking, prepare yourself a nice supple corn rig. I'm using a braided hooklink by Korda called 'SuperNatural'. It is perfect for a delicate corn rig.

05

With the aid of a knotless knot I have added a size 10 Wide Gape hook, and to the hair I have added 3 grains of corn taken out of my Pineapple slime corn.

06

Now you just need to tie up your Funnel web bag. I'm using the Original funnel web system in its all singing all dancing system. It's coded a yellow colour, so you know what size to look for in the tackle shops!

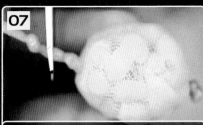

07

Follow the instructions and tie off a nice tight bag like so. Now cut between the two knots on the PVA.

08

All that's left to do now is hook the bag on and cast it out. This really is a devastating cold water tactic, give it a go.

BOILIE SOAK

When the weather is at its coldest and the fish really are not in the feeding mood, then casting an attractive single hookbait to different spots during a day, can pick up bonus fish rather than feeding one spot and concentrating your efforts there. It couldn't be easier to do.

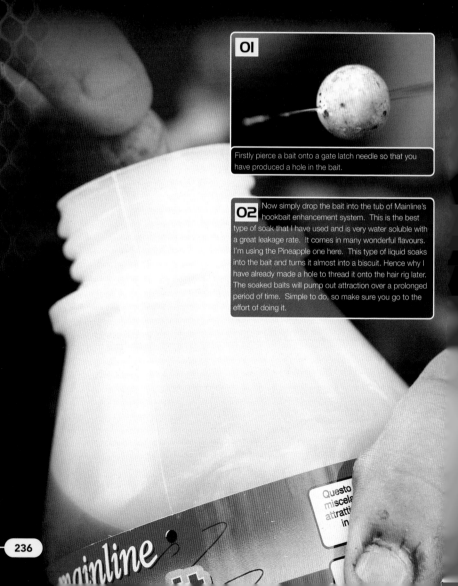

01

Firstly pierce a bait onto a gate latch needle so that you have produced a hole in the bait.

02 Now simply drop the bait into the tub of Mainline's hookbait enhancement system. This is the best type of soak that I have used and is very water soluble with a great leakage rate. It comes in many wonderful flavours. I'm using the Pineapple one here. This type of liquid soaks into the bait and turns it almost into a biscuit. Hence why I have already made a hole to thread it onto the hair rig later. The soaked baits will pump out attraction over a prolonged period of time. Simple to do, so make sure you go to the effort of doing it.

A BAG OF GOO!

This is probably the most underused tactic of them all, but for serious specimen hunters, this can really make a huge difference to your catch rate.

01 All you need is a tub of the hookbait enhancement system and a packet of solid PVA bags.

02 Now with your fingers keep the top of the bag open and then slowly pour in enough liquid to fill the bag half full.

03 It should look like so.

04 Now lick the top of the bag.

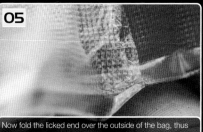

05 Now fold the licked end over the outside of the bag, thus closing the bag off.

06 Now put a few piercings with the aid of a small boilie needle into the PVA. This will help water attack the PVA when immersed in water. Then finally nick the hook into the corner of the bag. Now cast it to where you think the biggies are.

BOOSTED PELLETS

Using high oil pellets in winter can often work against you, purely because the water temperature doesn't allow them to disperse the attraction as positively as they would in the warmer months. Therefore giving your pellets a boost can make a great difference to your results.

01

Firstly add 3 handfuls of 4-8mm pellets into your bait tub

02

Next add a handful of Blitz multi-mix into the tub, mix this in so that you get a 'dusty' coat on all the pellets.

03

Next squirt in a good coating of the particle and pellet syrup. I'm using the Tiger nut version here.

04

Once everything is mixed in, the whole lot should look like so. When coupled with a PVA bag or catapulted out near your hookbait, the amount of attraction released will be awesome! The groundbait coating will also let off a cloudy scent from the pellets. A great tactic and something I suggest you all try when you next use pellets during the colder months.

SUMMARY

Hopefully over the last few pages you would have seen just how many options there are when using liquids. This really is tip of the iceberg stuff and maybe somewhere down the line we will bring you a few more tips on this subject. The liquids I have used in this chapter are ones that I rate very highly. They all taste good as well, which is very important. Some liquids on the market are too harsh and you just know they are more likely to 'repel' rather than 'attract' fish.

Having used them on this trip successfully through landing a beautiful mid-double, whilst stalking the channel that flanks the point that I was fishing, it proved once again how boosting your approach with liquids really WILL make a difference. In a short session, where everywhere has been fishing hard, I'm really pleased with my result.

HOOKBAITS

Sitting behind motionless indicators is the quickest route to jumping in the car and driving to the nearest Golf course. It doesn't breed confidence and certainly doesn't give you the required va va voom to want to go angling. I want to take you through a subject that is very close to my heart and an instrumental part in my success on the bank: Hookbaits.

Having surveyed hundreds of hours of underwater footage, during Korda's many jaunts domestically and in Europe filming our quarry underwater, I have seen first hand just how critical a change of hookbait can be in putting fish on the bank. The choice of hookbaits out there is monumental. Any visit into a tackle shop will reveal hundreds of options on the shelf. Also visits into the supermarket will open up a whole host of other great options. I dismiss very little in my fishing and choose the right hookbait to match the right situation. How do you make the right choices?

I can't emphasise enough how crucial your choice of hookbait can be in transforming a session, this can be so critical in turning pick-ups into full 'blooded' runs off angry carp. However buoyancy and hookbait weight is just one part of the equation. A number of other factors play an influential part in turning a quiet day into a great one.

COLOUR

Never underestimate just how instrumental colour can be in fishing success. Carp have extraordinary eye-sight, and as I explained previously I have been fortunate enough to sit glued to the underwater monitors and noticed the reaction of carp to a change in hookbait colour. One particular experience sticks out like a sore thumb in my memory. The day was a hot May day in France, the carp were spawning and nothing seemed like it wanted to feed. As Danny Fairbrass, Adam Penning and I watched intently, carp continued to circle our baited area by the underwater camera. On odd occasions, one would tilt down and experience a mouthful of our carpy feast, but never hard enough to allow them to get to our hookbait. The hookbait was then changed to a yellow one from the dark fishmeal based bottom bait. In the next 2 hours, that hookbait was picked up 5 times! If that doesn't prove a point nothing will. My favourite colours are Yellow and Orange, however other colours like White, Red and Pink are also very effective. So next time things are slow, bear this information in mind.

FLAVOURS

Like colour, the potency in smell of a hookbait can be an awesome catalyst for inducing action. I always try to use a hookbait that is slightly stronger in smell than my freebies. I feel that when fish move over a baited area, that food signal out of the hookbait needs to scream 'eat me'. Of course on some pressured venues where carp have seen every trick in the book, using more subtle smells can pay dividence, but on most standard lakes or day ticket venues, I always go for the high powered approach. Colour plus a strong food signal can really propel your results.

Once again, similarly to colour, if things aren't going to plan, tinker on one rod. Change the flavour and colour of hookbait and see how you fair? Some of the artificial hookbaits can be excellent, and the flavoured ones are extremely effective. I use the Enterprise tackle range and they really are excellent. The flavoured plastic corn, as a single hookbait on its own can be brilliant. Couple it with a PVA bag, and things will really hot up!

SHAPE

A very underestimated characteristic of a hookbait is shape. Carp are very used to round boilie shaped baits these days and will noticeably reject round baits as soon as they enter their mouth. Here's another mind-blowing example: on a particular underwater film shoot, we baited the camera every night before dark with a variety of bait, ready for the next days filming. On this particular occasion we decided to put out a few handfuls of round boilies along with our mixed particles, groundbait and chopped boilies. When the dust settled and the bait hit the bottom, we were able to count the number of round boilies, 47 was the number.

We chuckled at having counted them and went to socialise ready for the next days filming. The following morning we switched the camera's on just as the light was good enough for filming. The carp had cleaned up all the bait, but surprise surprise, all that remained was 47 round boilies! Unbelievable, the fish had moved the baits around, but had completely refused to eat them. This was a holiday venue in france with a good stock of fish. A more potent lesson you couldn't wish to learn! So the message is simple, try different shaped hookbaits on your visits to pressured day ticket venues, pellet shaped hookbaits, artificial corn, peanuts or dumbbell shaped boilies. These little changes will all add a few percent to your chances of success.

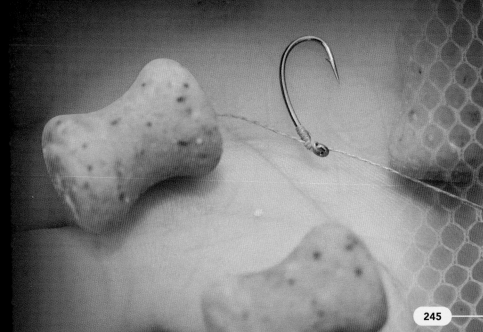

THE MUZZA

The first time I saw this rig, my mate Tom Dove was using it to great effect at Walthamstow reservoirs. He was fishing boilies, a favoured method of mine and catching loads. This particular rig really helps to make your hookbait behave as naturally as possible but also it helps to drop the hook point down into the carps mouth, because the buoyant nature of the cork helps lift the eye of the hook ever so slightly thus making the hook point drop down once the bait has been picked up, simple science!

01

With a bait drill the same diameter as your cork sticks, begin to slowly drill out the core of the bait.

02

Drill ¾ half of the way through the bait, but not the whole way.

03

A nice neat slot waiting for the cork plug.

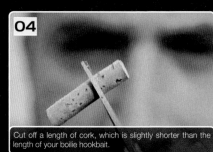

04

Cut off a length of cork, which is slightly shorter than the length of your boilie hookbait.

05

Thread the boilie onto the baiting needle so the un-drilled part of the boilie is threaded on first.

06

Now slide on your cork plug and push into the cavity in the boilie.

07

The rig is tied KD rig style as shown elsewhere in this book. Now thread on your hookbait.

08

Secure the bait in place with a boilie stop. Easy to do, but simple is often best!

SUMMARY

Well I hope that has given you a little insight into how important hookbaits are in my fishing. I spend hours rolling my own and pay a lot of thought to the hookbait for every situation. Wherever possible I try to match my hookbait to my freebies, in size. However colour and smell I try to vary and really impose the presence of my hookbait on my baited area. It really can make a difference. The pictures have shown you some of my favourites and how I like to capitalise on using them. Give them a go, match your hookbait to every situation, and remember, if it isn't happening, RING THE CHANGES!

A beautiful 47lb 8oz common caught on the 'muzza'.

HI VIZ HOOKBAITS

This chapter is focused on giving you a guide through Hi-Visual baits. Hookbaits play a very critical part in my fishing, and they are a component that can transform a bad days fishing into a very productive one. One of my top hookbait choices is a bright smelly hi-visual one and throughout this chapter I'll be giving you advice and tips on my favourite ones.

Hi-Visual carp baits saw a massive rise during the late nineties. I was fortunate to be on the pulse of the phenomenon as I was fishing a lake called Redesmere in Cheshire and my now good friend Frank Warwick was ripping the venues in the area to pieces on his bright highly flavoured single hookbaits. In fact I moved up North during 1998 and these guys had been using these baits regularly for over 8 years, it took so long for the rest of country to catch on. I wonder how many carp, people missed out on by not using these baits. Since those early days during the late nineties things have developed tenfold and the number of companies that have started thanks to Franks early innovations is unbelievable! I say Frank because he was the first guy I knew of that went down the bright

food route with quite exceptional results. This style of fishing certainly added a new dimension to my angling and if you ever catch me fishing without a tub of my favourite Hi-viz baits in my ruck sack then I'll give you everything I own. I really have that much faith in them.

Bright baits have evolved somewhat now, so much so that we are inundated with all manner of wonderful colours, flavours and artificial alternatives. The Hi-Viz side of debates has induced so much research and you would only have to visit google on the internet or ask Jeeves and enter words like "carp vision" or "What spectrum do Carp see" and you will be inundated with essay after essay from biological professors commenting and delivering hypothesis after hypothesis on their detailed research into "light refraction" and the "colours that carp see". It really is a can of worms that I haven't got the words to explain or bore you with, but what I will bore you with is the facts and more importantly, THE RESULTS.

Hi-Viz baits are an option that no angler should go fishing without. On days when nothing else is working, a single hookbait bait fished on its own can produce the goods. I have developed my favourites over the years, and I'm sure once you start putting them through their paces you too will reap the rewards. The picture sequences will give you a guide to different colours and flavours. Another thing worth mentioning is that once you have developed a touch of confidence with these baits it will be worth buying some base mix and making your own single hookbaits at a later stage to develop your own touch of uniqueness!

Bright baits are invariably heavily flavoured, far more flavoured than a standard boilie in a kilo bag. The reason for this is that you should never feed your hookbaits as freebies. Just to give you an idea, 1kg of normal bagged boilies will contain around 3-6ml of flavour plus other additives. It will take around 8 size 2 eggs to make a kilo of boilies. In a single hookbait such as a tub of one of my all time favourites, Mainlines Pineapple pop-ups, you are likely to have 8ml of flavour per egg. That means there is about 8 times more flavour (minimum) in a single hookbait compared to a 'freebie'.

Flavour alone will generally have a bitter taste and this is levelled up with sweetners in base mixes of boilies, however even with such additions it would have an adverse effect to feed baits with such high concentrations of flavour, however as a single hookbait over less obtrusive bait or alone they are absolutely devastating, both from a visual perspective and smell. The best way to describe it is like soap! You wouldn't eat it, but some of those smells coming out of 'Lush' or the 'Body shop' are awesome, good enough to eat, you get the picture!

I have witnessed such amazing reactions to my bright pop-ups. I have seen fish refuse a bait hard on the bottom and subtle in smell, close in the margins. However I have then presented a bright yellow pop-up in-front of the same fish and they have snapped it up in an instant, quite unbelievable to witness.

A COLOURFUL GUIDE

The world has gone visual baits mad these days, so many colours, smells and shapes. the following pictures and captions should help point you in the right direction when it comes to making the right choices in the right situation.

I really rate this lazy pop-up rig as it adds an element to the rig that makes it very difficult for the carp to deal with. The shot on the hair allows the hook to behave like it should and is not affected by the buoyant bait. The size 10 Korda Wide Gape hook should sit on its side on the bottom with the boilie just 'wafting' about above it.

These are 3 of my favourite pop-up flavours and types. You won't go far wrong with these.

My tub of different shapes and sizes of artificial baits go with me everywhere. I really rate them and I have had mine soaking in Mainline Baits Peach-ade for ages. This allows them to soak in some flavour and gives me a little 'edge' I think.

With just a nice hooklink material an array of hooks and a tub of mixed shot you can do so many things to alter your presentation to allow you to get the best out of every given session.

Yellow is still my favourite colour and coupled with pineapple flavour it is deadly all your round, I have genuinely lost count of how many fish I have caught on yellow pineapple baits. They truly are the millenniums tutti frutti. Coupled with the shot on the hair rig that just sinks the bait you have a devastating combination.

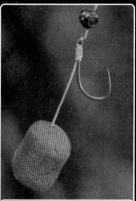

Don't just stick to one shape, on waters that receive a lot of angling pressure try to vary the shape of your hookbait. Just a simple change in bait shape can induce a bite! Here I am using a pink plum pop-up, after yellow I have had the most success with pink. On days when yellow has been slow, a quick change to a bright pink bait can induce a bite. On this rig I have a small shot behind the eye of the hook, which just sinks the hook and bait, this gives me a pop-up no higher than the size of my hook. Give it a try you won't be disappointed.

No one said that fluoro baits can't be mixed with dark baits to give a varied presentation. The scent of the darker food bait coupled with the visual impact of an artificial piece of corn can score superbly well and is a brilliant tactic when fishing over beds of particles or pellet and when you want to present a bottom bait with a fleck of colour in them.

I used to be sceptical regarding how good fake corn is just fished on its own as a single hookbait and unflavoured! I shouldn't have worried, I don't know what it is, but fish cannot resist these. Green and Blue are two of the most visible colours to carp especially in deep water. Fake corn can be purchased in both sinking and floating versions. Enterprise Tackle have a great range and are the company that I prefer for my artificial hookbaits.

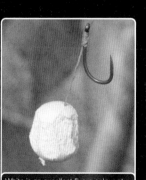

White is an excellent fluoro colour at night. Sometimes bright baits can slow down when darkness strikes, however my experiences have always shown that white baits can work all night. Milky toffee and chocolate malts are all time classics and generally come in white versions. It is also a great colour when zig rig fishing. Bear that in mind.

Fluoro orange is one of bright hookbait innovator Frank Warwick's favourites. Scopex and tutti frutti are two of the 'killer baits' in this colour. A nice 1-inch pop-up can often produce bites when fish are not interested in a mass baiting approach. A single pop-up fished with a PVA bag can produce wonders.

Fake bread with the shot on the hair rig coupled with a PVA Funnel web stick of bread crumb is both Hi-visual and irresistible. Give it a try on weedy waters.

Two pieces of bright yellow fake corn is one of my all time favourite zig rig hookbaits. When the weather is scorching hot and you can't buy a bite. fish one a foot under the surface with this hookbait on and get ready for a screaming run!

A single piece of fake maize threaded on long ways onto the hair is bright and small, ideal for small and pressured carp.

Just something worth remembering. Whether you are fishing for roach or big carp a bright bait will score well. Additionally no matter how big the bait is to start with, you can always cut it down to match the hook size you are using no matter how small. By slowly trimming the bait down, you can get it to slowly sink with the weight of the hook giving you a beautiful slow sinking presentation.

BRIGHT AND SMELLY

On short sessions you often won't need much more than a hi-visual hookbait coupled with a smelly stick mix that will lure patrolling carp in the area. The following stick mix is one I love and use very often. It's not only visual but extremely attractive. Firstly with the aid of the Korda Krusha, chop about 20 boilies of different colours and smells into a small bait tub.

01
Add a generous handful of Hinders Mini Pellet combo and some 4mm Mainline response pellet to some crushed Hi-visual bottom baits.

02
Now add a tin of tuna in brine to this lot. Tuna is one of the best PVA bag ingredients you can get buy, its cheap and there isn't a fish on this planet that swims, that won't ravage tuna!

03
Now mix the Tuna in with the bright boilie crumb and pellet.

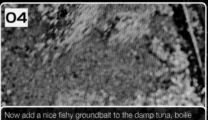

04
Now add a nice fishy groundbait to the damp tuna, boilie crumb and pellet, the groundbait will soak in the brine and leave you with a lovely PVA friendly mix.

05
Give it a good mix.

06
You should be left with a lovely coarse mix that will breakdown into a lovely pile of goodness. It should not be sticky and should not stick to itself!

07

Now using the 'Longchuck' Funnel web system, tie off a lovely compressed stick. The instructions are on the front of the Korda tube. If you haven't used Funnel web then you are missing out on some awesome fishing!

08

I always have a loop on the end of my hooklength. Latch this onto a gated baiting needle that already has my small 1inch PVA stick threaded on.

09

Then thread the PVA stick down the hooklink and gently pull the hookpoint into the stick, whilst ensuring that you have no big bits in your PVA mix that could mask your hookpoint.

10

Now all you have to do is clip it onto you 'Stik Klip' on your lead clip using the loop at the end of your hooklink.

11

This one fell for the slow sinking cut down apple-core shaped Pink Fruit-tella option. All colours have their days based on the lake and the conditions, just follow my tips and you won't go far wrong.

Today has been NO different, I have literally struggled to keep a rod in the water and my combination of different shaped buoyant baits with different colours and flavours has produced excellent results. Gareth Purnell the photographer was quite shocked to see how every other angler on the lake was catching nothing yet my two rods baited with different Hi-Viz options struggled to be kept in the water such was the intensity of the bites.

My PVA stick and bright bait combo was taking the lake by storm. I had some 15 carp in a matter of a few hours which shows just how good this approach can be. I put absolutely NO free bait out and fished with just the bright bags and Korda Longchuck Funnel web sticks. Bites where instant and I couldn't have demonstrated the approach anymore convincingly. Follow the pictures and make sure you apply the ideas and rig ideas to your fishing. You will not be disappointed.

WONDER BAITS

From the moment I smelt Frank Warwick's bright round balls of goodness I was hooked! From that day on, making my own custom hookbaits became a massive element of my fishing and not only that, it contributed a major edge to my results that would help to transform often bleak days into barnstormers.

Moving up North in 1998 and meeting some of the awesome anglers on the banks of Redesmere in Cheshire opened my eyes to a whole new dimension in my fishing. Talking to Frank over the years and also Steve Morgan at Mainline baits opened up a whole new can of worms in my fishing and I have become obsessed over the years in producing my own little 'specials' to separate my fishing and results from the pack. I rate this so highly that after 11 years I think it's about time I pass some of these little secrets over to you. Over the coming chapters I will guide you through exactly how to produce your own custom hookbaits that will make you the envy of all your angling friends.

BRIGHT, POTENT AND DEADLY!

In this chapter I'm guiding you through one of my secret recipe's that till today has rarely been in print. These have caught thousands of carp for my friends and I. They have been so successful, that I now have a waiting list in the Korda office for them! My rule is that once you've been working at Korda for over a year, you qualify to enter the waiting list! So consider yourself lucky!

If you haven't yet used a hi-visual hookbait, where have you been? They can be quite simply explosive. I wouldn't even like to guess how many carp I have caught on these in the last ten years, but I'm pretty convinced that without them I wouldn't have caught half as many.

A special hookbait and a funnel web bag has caught me countless carp.

WONDER BAITS

The mix I have covered in this chapter is really easy to do, but more importantly, it's an explosive combination of flavours that combines two wonderful elements that will work 12 months of the year. I'm a great fan of the Citrus and Berry combination. The Tangerine Oil and the Pineapple flavour give it a beautiful rounded profile that will electrify fish into action, whilst the Berry type smell in the Fruit-tella gives the bait a deep longing smell that is simply irresistible! I can't rave on enough about how good this mix is, just try it for yourself.

01 It might look like a lot of bottles, but trust me they're all there for a reason.

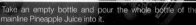
02 Take an empty bottle and pour the whole bottle of the mainline Pineapple Juice into it.

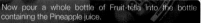
03 Now pour a whole bottle of Fruit-tella into the bottle containing the Pineapple juice.

04 This time pour half the bottle of Tangerine oil into the bottle with the other two flavours.

05 Now add Sweet-Ade. I always add sweetner at a ratio of 2:5. So 2ml of sweetener to every 5ml of flavour.

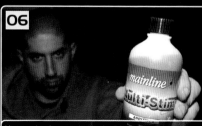
06 Your previously empty bottle should now be half full of flavour and sweetner, now top up the bottle by half with Multi-stim.

07

Give the whole lot a shake and savour the flavour! This will be your flavour and bait soak for many months to come.

08

Now crack a large egg into a mixing bowl.

09

Add half a table spoon of Yellow dye.

10

Give the whole lot a good mix.

11

I now add 30ml of flavour from my mixed bottle of goodness.

12

Bit by bit, add your Mainline Polaris pop-up mix.

13

You should be left with a nice firm dough that is pliable and not too dry.

14

I have repeated the process this time with white dye so I can have multi-coloured baits.

15

Cover a tray with a light coating of pop-up mix to stop your rolled baits from sticking to the tray.

16

You can now either roll your baits by hand or on a bait roller, but don't be afraid to make some different shapes and sizes.

17

Boil in small batches for approx 90-120 seconds. The bigger your baits the longer you will need to boil them for.

18

Remove from the boiling water and lay onto a tea towel, this will soak up the excess moisture.

Now leave the baits to air dry away from any damp places for two weeks, in which time they should be really hard and ready for a soaking.

THE RE-HYDRATION SECRET

Probably the most important element of making these single hookbaits is what you do with them once they've been boiled. This is a major edge that my friends and I have been incorporating for years and it definitely makes a huge difference. If you follow the picture sequence, you will notice that all the flavours are poured into one big bottle, which is your flavour concoction. This is then emulsified and diluted with Mainlines Multi-stim, which is an awesome appetite stimulant. Once you have dried your baits out on a towel in a cool dry place for 1-2 weeks, you then put the baits in a tub and glaze them with a drizzle of the liquid from this bottle.

Once they soak that up, add some more and just keep repeating this process over the coming weeks and months. What you will find is that these baits will just get better and better as they absorb more and more attraction into their core. They really become potent, but because of the sweet ade content, they are never too over powering, which ensures they remain attractive to fish from the second they enter the water to the minute they are gulped into a carp's mouth. Remember to give the bottle a good shake whenever you go to give your baits a soak. This ensures that all the different elements are nicely mixed together.

My UK PB (40lb 10oz) taken on a snowman using wonderbaits and Mainline Cell.

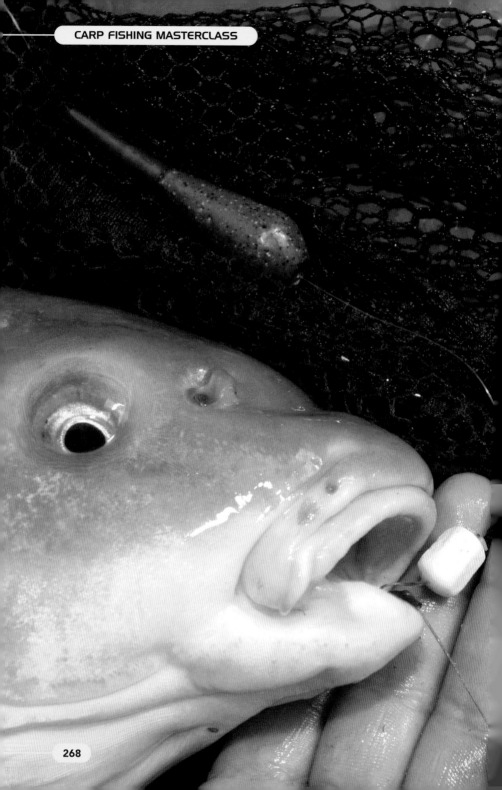

A BIT OF ALL WHITE

For the next instalment in my hookbait chapters, I will be looking at adjusting 'food bait boilies'. I have been using the Cell by Mainline baits for over 2 years now, and hand on heart I can safely say that along with the Activ-8, it's the best boilie I have ever used. No matter where I've fished with it, it has produced brilliant results for my friends and I. Unlke some food baits, the Cell is both a great long term choice, but also a great instant bait that will catch on venue's from the off.

When fishing over the Cell, similarly to any type of boilie, it's always worth giving your hookbait its own unique identity or just a small tweak that can transform a slow day into a good one. So why change a perfectly good boilie at all? There are a number of reasons why I do this, and I think they're all worth considering because depending on angling pressure and the mood that the carp are in, giving your hookbait an 'edge' WILL make the difference.

REASONS FOR CHANGE
- Fish on pressured venues often spook off fresh bait
- Giving the hookbait extra 'wow' factor
- Boosting flavour levels
- Adjusting the buoyancy

So how do I change my food bait hookbaits? This is really easy to do and something that I recommend you all do. One of the key components that I add is 'white' dye. This alone will give your hookbait mix an added dimension. The white colour is a great edge in itself and really makes your hookbait stand out on the bottom. This is exceptionally good when the carp are not in a major feeding mood, because as long as they move over your baited area, they will spot that little bright white bait before anything else. I have seen it on many occasions when a carp moves over a baited area and snares the brightest food item immediately, even if it has less attraction.

The other great thing about the white colour is that it can make the hookbait resemble a 'washed out' Cell hookbait. When pale baits like the cell have been in the water for a long time, they then wash out quickly and turn a very pale cream/white. Washed out baits are often more attractive to carp, simply because they appear safer. Therefore not only is the white hookbait bright, it can often seem a safer option to the carp than one straight out of the readymade freezer bag. It's a colour that I really rate and an element that you can add to any base mix, whether it's the Activ-8, the Grange or a birdfood bait.

CREATE YOUR BIT OF ALL 'WHITE'!

This is so simple to do, that any of you can do this. With some colour and pop-up mix you can transform a normal standard boilie into an all singing all dancing hookbait which will make you stand out from the crowd.

01 These are the components you will be requiring.

02 Scoop four cupfuls of Cell Base Mix into a polythene bag.

03 Follow this with two cupfuls of Polaris Pop-Up Mix.

04 Thoroughly shake the contents, like so.

05 Crack open two eggs into a clean mixing bowl.

06 Now add 15ml of Cell Activator liquid.

07

Follow this with 15ml of Multi-Stim Additive.

08

A teaspoon of Mainline White will colour the hook bait.

09

When everything is added, your concoction will look like an all-day breakfast!

10

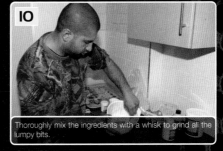

Thoroughly mix the ingredients with a whisk to grind all the lumpy bits.

11

Now add the mixture of your base mix and pop-up mix.

12

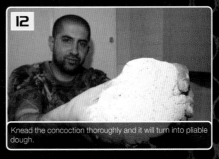

Knead the concoction thoroughly and it will turn into pliable dough.

13

If it's too stodgy, simply add more mix. If done correctly, it should be easy to form a ball but slightly sticky to the touch.

14

Pull off a small segment and begin to roll into a boilie shape.

15

Sprinkle some mix onto a tray. This prevents the baits from sticking.

16

Using a sieve, leave the boilies to boil for 1 minute and drain the excess water.

17

You can also wrap the paste around cork if you're a fan of chod rigs!

18

Finally, roll them carefully on a towel to remove moisture.

19

The Korda ready-rigs come in a variety of patterns and sizes.

20

They're perfectly formed and include a size 8 ring swivel tied to one end.

21

The hook section includes some silicone tubing to hold your bait in place.

22

Thread your balanced hook bait onto the hair of the rig.

23

Fix the hook bait in place incorporating a boilie stop or Extenda Stop.

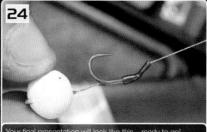

24

Your final presentation will look like this – ready to go!

If you follow the picture sequence you will notice how easy this is to do. I add 15ml of the Cell catalyst and then add Multi-stim as well, which is an appetite stimulant. This changes the food signal a little and gives it an added boost. When you smell the baits, you won't be able to tell the difference, but trust me the carp can. Small 'tinkerings' can really tap into the carps amazing sense of smell and colour.

You will also notice, that I have added Polaris pop-up mix to the base mix. I have added 33% to 66% Cell base mix or in mathematical terms 1:2! You won't notice these being much different in buoyancy, but trust me again when I say the subtle difference can make all the difference. It just takes the edge off the weight of the hook. If you want to make them more buoyant then increase the ratio's, to maybe 2:1 Polaris to Cell base mix. Do what suits your fishing. Additionally by rolling some chop shaped ones as shown, coupled with the slightly more buoyant bait, these are perfect for fishing over spod mix and Cell chops.

As you can see, even by making such small changes, you're giving your hookbait a number of advantages over a 'standard' bait out the bag, food for thought. Having got the baits rolled, I was super keen to take them out and put them through their paces, along with the Korda ready rigs. I was due to go on a shoot for Tight lines on Sky Sports, this was going to take place on the Grand Union canal in Hertfordshire.

I got there with my mate Tom Dove before the Sky camera's had arrived.
I received an immediate take on the new hookbaits, but the thing fell off. It was my fault for putting on an old rig rather than a fresh one or one of the new ready rigs, which are as good as anything I've ever seen tied.

Unfortunately that day turned into one big disaster with the filming commotion, coupled with untimely boat traffic putting pay to our days canal carping. However such was my faith I agreed to put the baits right back under the spotlight with a very short stalking trip planned. Whilst launching some new products at Cudmore in Staffordshire, I had a chance to go stalking on one of the carp lakes. I had an hour to catch one before having to set-off, the pressure was really on now! After baiting up a few marginal spots with a mixture of chop boilie and pellet, I planted myself at the end of a small bay. I lowered the little white cell bait down along with a small PVA bag just by a marginal snag. With the clutch set and line sunk, it was now time to see how good these baits really are! Just like the Canal, it didn't take long at all, after just 10 mins and the rest of the anglers on the lake blanking, my one rod was off to a flyer. After a spirited fight I slid the net under a beautiful common carp! Job done.

I can't rate these white cell hookbaits highly enough, these small tweaks can be incorporated into any base mix of your choice and once again its only limited by your imagination......they really are; a bit of all white!

GETTING STEAMY

Once carp have spawned, I have learnt to understand that a 'salty' bait with plenty of attraction can be just the ticket when you're searching for a quick bite. I always add salt and chilli to my spod mixes, so why not boilies for a bit of extra boost? The next requirement for a bait during the summer, is something that isn't too heavy and won't just sink like a brick to the bottom and find itself enveloped in weed.

I like to chop baits up so they flutter to the bottom, but imagine if the inherent ingredients in the mix, helped to slow the descent of the bait to the bottom? One last edge would be a bait that had the same attraction levels as a ball of paste but still had a skin on it so it couldn't be whittled down by nuisance fish. Without sounding cheesy, this bait does exist and can easily be made by any of you, in rapid quick time and with very little effort.

So what is it I hear you ask? Last year on a Korda fishing trip to France, one of the boys at Korda, Jonny Mann, reminded me of a method I used to use years ago, he had prepared them himself for that very trip, it triggered something in my head and made me wonder why I hadn't used these 'special' baits more regularly during my fishing. I had named the bait 'steamies', and these are what I'm covering this chapter in a simple step-by-step sequence. I have chosen to use the now legendary Mainline Activ-8 as the base, with a few added tit bits that give it a unique edge.

On its own the Activ is superb, but I have included some other items to boost the salt levels and also enhance their buoyancy a little. They're so easy to make, I've actually taken the ingredients on the bank with me, and not only am I going to make them on the bank, I'm also going to cast one straight out to prove just how devastatingly effective they are. I mentioned a couple of extra ingredients, today I'm using the dried shrimp and insect meal and this is available from CC moore's, which gives the bait not only buoyancy, but also additional salty attraction. By stirring these into the egg's and Activator liquid as shown, you help hydrate them, but because of the inherent buoyancy of these ingredients, it really helps to slow the descent of your bait down onto the lake bed, making them ideal for use over silt or silk weed.

Are you wondering what separates these from a normal boilie? The key is in the boiling process. Instead of the baits being made into round shapes on a roller and then dropped into boiling water, the paste that is boosted and laced with goodness is rolled into sausages. These sausages are then wrapped in cling film, then dropped into the boiling water for 10 minutes, but you can boil them for longer if you wish. The boiling method completely separates these from a standard boilie, because unlike a standard boilie that has a percentage of its attraction boiled out, these lose little or no attraction as all the goodness is contained within the cling film, therefore you don't boil any of the Activator and other amazing attractors out the bait.

MAKING STEAMIES

Rolling your own boilies can be a pain and a lengthy process if you've never done it before. However making steamies is easy, quick and gives you plenty of room to experiment. It's so easy I'm doing them on the bankside. I've chosen ingredients that I really like, but it's not limited to these, you can go to town, as you can be sure every bit of goodness will be locked inside these steamies and not washed out during the boiling process.

01

The ingredients I'm using are Activ-8 base mix, Activator liquid, sea salt and some CC moore's shrimp and crustacean mix. Also CLING FILM, very important.

02

Crack 4 medium sized eggs into your mixing bowl or bucket.

03

Whisk your eggs.

04

Put in a handful maldon's sea salt into the eggs.

05

Add 15ml of Activator liquid to the eggs. The exact measure is also indicated on the Activator bottle.

06

Now add a couple of generous handfuls of the CC moore shrimp and crustacean mix.

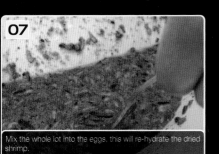

07

Mix the whole lot into the eggs, this will re-hydrate the dried shrimp.

08

Begin to add the activator base mix little by little.

09

Knead the mix so it is firm but ever so slightly sticky to touch.

10

Here is the finished ball of goodness ready for rolling.

11

Roll the ball into 4 or 5 even sized sausages.

12

Sausages at the ready

13

Now wrap your sausages into cling film.

14

Sausages all wrapped and ready for boiling.

15

Drop them into boiling water for 10-15minutes.

16

Once boiled being careful not to burn yourself, unwrap the cling film.

17

Firstly cut the cylinders into circles.

18

Then into cubes.

In a few minutes you'll have a sessions worth of bait ready to catch some carp! These look amazing if I do say so myself.

HYBRID LEADCLIP RIG

On today's session I'm putting the Korda ready rigs through their paces. I want to use the Hybrid lead clip leaders, so I'm going to have to adapt the rigs slightly to make them more interchangeable with this set-up.

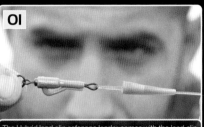

01

The Hybrid lead clip safezone leader comes with the lead clip already on the loop ready for use. Brilliant!

02

With wire cutters, take off the ring from the swivel at the end of the lead clip.

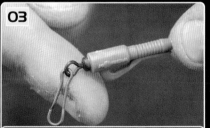

03

Replace with a stick clip.

04

I'm using the size 8 Wide Gape supernatural ready rig.

05

Cut the swivel off the ring on the rig.

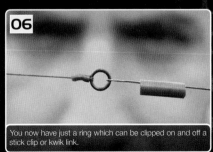

06

You now have just a ring which can be clipped on and off a stick clip or kwik link.

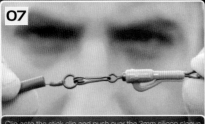

07 Clip onto the stick clip and push over the 3mm silicon sleeve to secure in place.

08 At the other end, thread on a steamie cube and secure in place with an extenda stop which comes complete with a ready rig.

09 The rig is ready to go, but one last touch!

IO Hook on a small funnel web bag of pellets and a couple of steamies.

I'm introducing the rig along the marginal reeds with an Angling Intelligence 12m pole.

A bite within 5 minuites of positioning
my rigs and I'm not joking.

The proof is simple just look at the colour of the water once you've made your bait, there's no surface scum and brown water, it's generally good enough to drink. Once these sausages have been boiled, it's a simple case of unwrapping the cling film and then cutting these into the required sizes of cubes. Could it be any simpler? I do agree that these can't be used in a throwing stick, but apart from that, they can be used in a catapult or spod mix, or in today's case introduced via the Angling Intelligence margin pole! When these are finished you can smell the goodness straight away, and even the carp agree. On today's session I'm at a small club water, with some excellent margin fishing to be had.

With the baits finished I set about introducing them, in a short day session, the action was frantic and the baits clearly adored by the carp, no surprise really when you think about what's in them. 8 bites off some angry mid double mirrors was a job well done! I utilised the new Korda ready rigs as they came complete with extenda stops, so I could vary the hookbait size without having to change the rig! The hookholds were immense even in a hit and hold situation.

If you're after a bait that will separate you from the man next door and a bait that will get you instant bites then give these a try. You have all the inherent attractions of paste, but the skin of a boilie, they're quick to make, and give you plenty of options to experiment. Go in search of your inner Gordan Ramsay!

RELEASE YOUR
POTENTIAL

RDA - Tackle for heroes.

KORDA.CO.UK
FOR THE THINKING BEHIND THE TACKLE

CANAL CAPERS

My love affair with canals started somewhat bizarrely back in 1999/2000. At the time I had only been living in the Northwest for a couple of years and most of my fishing was concentrated on the difficult Mere's with a very low stock of carp. There are very few waters in the North West where you can go and bag a few fish of a decent size in a day. Most are oversubscribed busy day ticket venues and that wasn't my cup of tea. So where could I go to unwind and catch a couple of doubles in a day?

Around the same time, one of my good friends that I had met fishing the mighty Redesmere moved home, much closer to the village that I lived in. His new home just happened to be aptly positioned on the banks of the Trent & Mersey Canal in Northwich. Both of us knew little about this stretch, but we were aware of a decent head of carp in other parts of this canal. I remember our first exploration exercise like it was only yesterday. I popped over to Chris' house at around 9pm in the evening after finishing a shift at the pub I worked in whilst being a poor student. It was a Saturday evening so Match of the day was on shortly, so we went about positioning a rod for a 'laugh' right in front of his living room window, we laughed like little kids about our 'window spot'.

The rod positioned tight against the marginal 'overgrown' grass was then baited with a handful of boilies and the trap was set. As we sat down for our rather bizarre experience of fishing and football wrapped into one evening, we both remarked how amazing it would be if this stretch of canal held any carp!! After about 30 minutes, the bite alarm receiver let out a single bleep, which registered in his living where we were sat. A dual comical 'oooooh' left our lips.

However nothing was to prepare us for what followed as some 5 minutes later the single rod sat in-front of the living room window burst into frantic life, with the buzzer shrieking in disapproval at what was on the end and the real spinning at a rate of knots! We both shot off the couch and rushed in an Olympic style race for the rod, Chris being the home owner called rank and grabbed the rod, and after a typical spirited canal fight I slipped the net under a lovely mid double! It was one of those magical fishing moments that will stay with me forever, but it also taught me a lesson, if you want bites in bad conditions then check out canals!

Over the next few years we enjoyed many a happy night on canals bagging good fish, and I also explored other stretches in the Northwest catching well from them all. The Bridgewater, Shropshire Union and The Trent & Mersey were truly prolific venues which filled a void in my fishing up North by giving me somewhere to go and get a bend in my rod away from the pressures of 'Big carp hunting'.

I have now lived down south for 4 years and have not set foot on a canal since my days up north, but I was keen to prove that even in the worst conditions a canal can produce a carp, but also to demonstrate the methods and approach you need to fool them! I was very apprehensive about this challenge as I hate going somewhere that I have never seen before, especially in the depths of winter, but after a few phone calls, my mate Nick Helleur suggested a wonderful stretch of canal situated in Wilstone, Tring, which belongs to Tring Anglers and is also available on day ticket.

The morning was blessed with -2 temperatures but promising a sunny winter day. As I set foot on the crunchy frosted grass, my eyes were greeted by a beautiful short stretch of canal that had a far bank littered with dense foliage and snags. If carp would be anywhere, it would be here. The area screamed carp, but would they bite? I was hoping that my canal instincts would come flooding back to me, so that I could at least fool one fish on this potentially tricky day.

LOCATION

People sometimes think that canals have a low density of fish and that they can't be prolific. You couldn't be further from the truth, many canals in this country are rammed with fish, and I'm surprised that they haven't been a more fashionable choice of venue. This particular stretch looks awesome and is a little more snaggy than stretches that I have fished in the past. Because snags made up the far margin on so much of this 'lock' I needed to look for what posed the best chance. Moored boats and cover on canals with little 'foliage' can be dead certainties for those of you that are up for the challenge, as are bends, and wides (areas built for boats to turn), these all hold carp. On this particular session I was looking for dense snags, and also how far they protrude from the far bank. My chosen plot was almost half way along this lock. I set up slightly up stream from where I am going to place my rigs, but I did this so that I could spread my baits along the stretch a little.

After I walked along the stretch a little I highlighted 2-3 areas that I would position my baits in. All 3 where tight against the snags but they all looked excellent, my confidence was building.

CANAL RIG

Canals are renowned for bottom debris, shopping trolleys, bottles, cars, and much more have been known to litter canal beds! This particular stretch appears to be in a more affluent area of the country, so I don't think I will be contending with car engines or trolleys, but nonetheless the snags carry enough threat for me to have to fish heavy and cleverly.

01

Slide on a Korda Safezone tail rubber onto your mainline or Safezone leader

02

Next thread on your Korda Safezone lead clip.

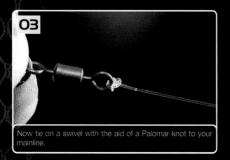

03

Now tie on a swivel with the aid of a Palomar knot to your mainline.

04

Pull the lead clip over the swivel and pull until it 'clicks', this means it will work effectively, should the lead become snagged whilst playing a fish.

05

Now add a small 2oz Korda flat swivel pear lead.

06

Finally slide over your tail rubber over around 4 teeth on the lead clip. Do not push it over too tightly otherwise the fish has no chance of getting rid of the lead if you lose the fish. All that's left to do now is tie on your hooklink to the swivel.

I'm using strong hooks today to counter the snags and general dangers, the fight off a powerful carp is bound to be intense so a hook like a Korda Wide Gape is a must have.

Finally a strong 20lb plus hooklink is important.

With my lead discharge system and a strong hook arrangement to compliment my terminal set-up, I'm confident that I have the right tackle to combat these powerful canal carp.

CANAL BAIT

Next on the agenda was bait, having fished canals in the past during the winter, I knew that bright smelly hookbaits were always successful, so these are my choice of hookbait, coupled with a PVA bag of pellets and 10mm Mainline Cell boilies. However I felt with the cold temperatures, I would need something to give the carp a little wake up call and get them sniffing around the outside of the snags. I have always found this a great tactic on canals, especially in the winter, so along with my sprinkling of 10mm Mainline Cell boilies I planned on introducing a couple of groundbait balls on each spot, to get both silver fish interested which would develop a 'feeding pyramid' for the carp to come in on. A feeding pyramid, is a process, where you feed your swim in a manner that will get smaller silver fish feeding. The frenzied response and clouding of the water that is generated by these fish, then lures larger specimens such as carp.

01

Firstly add half a bag of Voodoo groundbait, this is very meaty and smelly, ideal for what we are trying to achieve today.

02

Next add a few handfuls of Mainlines Activated Nut mix, this will compliment the meaty aroma nicely.

03

Add a few handfuls of Hinders Mixed pellet

04

Add a few handfuls of chopped and whole Mainline cell boilies.

05

Finally add half a tin of corn plus juice to the mix.

06

Mix with water until it will hold together enough to be under-armed to the various fishing spots, but I want my groundbait to still break up on impact with the water to give me that cloud effect.

LINE CONCEALMENT

An important thing to remember on any canal is that your fishing room is very small, both where you're fishing and where you're set-up. The first thing to remember is to leave ample room between your rods and fishing chair, so that dog walkers, cyclists, joggers and pleasure walkers all have room to pass without potentially kicking your rods into orbit by accident!! This means positioning your rods at an angle to the waters edge, generally pointing up stream or downstream towards your baited rigs. On this session mine are pointing downstream towards the different positions that my rigs are placed. This particular bit of canal doesn't look like it gets too much boat traffic, but in other stretches barges are rife with happy captain 'pugwashes' 12 months of the year. This can be a real pain if you don't conceal your lines when carp fishing as it means winding in every half hour or so as a boat passes or risk having the boats wipe out your line and strip your reels of line! Not a pleasant experience but it can be cured with the aid of backleads.

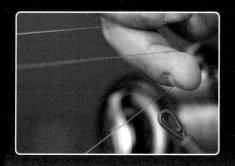 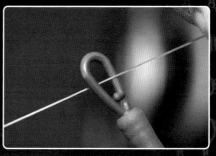

FISH ACTION

It's important on canals to remain quite mobile. If fish are there, very often you will catch them when they decide to feed. Therefore I set myself a target for the day. If I didn't get action by 1pm, I would go and explore some other stretches of canal. Because I'm travelling light, this would be easy to do. Like River fishing, it pays to be mobile on canals and explore different places, especially when it's freezing cold. However with the beautiful winter sun on my back, I wasn't surprised when my middle rod slammed into action and I was bent into my first canal carp in over 4 years! Old habits die hard and the adrenaline came flooding back! However no sooner had I hit the heady heights of excitement that I came sliding back to reality when the line dropped slack and the fish was gone.

The lead had discharged effectively but my hooklink had been sheared on one of the sharp snags. I was gutted, but inspired by the quick action, which convinced me that I was in the right area. As the day progressed I continued to trickle small handfuls of 10mm boilies over the spot, this acted as a drip feed to supplement the balls of groundbait down in the abyss. As the day was drawing to a close, I notified Gareth Purnell the photographer who had been keen to stay, that 'DUSK' is a great time on canals. On many occasions a lifeless stretch of canal comes alive at this time and today was no different.

Out of nowhere, my left hand rod positioned some 40yards down stream burst into life, with the line tightening in typical carp fashion. Bizarre resistance met my strike and surprisingly the culprit was a skimmer that would be lucky to hit 8oz!! I quickly positioned my rod back on the spot and noticed a big patch of bubbles appear when I under-armed my rig in. That was no skimmer that just spooked off that spot! No sooner had I placed the rod on the rest that my other rod burst into life again. I was lucky to be close to the rod and as soon as I struck into it, I knew I had an angry carp on the end. With the severe snags to contend with, I started walking back. When snag fishing its important not to wind when you hook your fish, WALK BACK, this is far more effective, and doesn't give the fish any unnecessary slack line to snag you with.

All I did was walk back until I saw the fish swirl on the perimeter of the snags and I knew the worst of the fight had been dealt with! Using the right tackle was important and after a few short bursts of power under the rod tip the fish was safely in the folds of the net!! I was ecstatic with the result and coming through a difficult challenge in tricky conditions on a brand new venue that I've never fished! The beautiful old warrior of a common glistened like a bar of gold in the dying light.

CONCLUSIONS

This was a lovely reminder of the wonderful sessions that I enjoyed on canals. They truly are one of the hidden gems of British waterways. I know that some places can be sketchy to fish, but if you have a root about, you're sure to discover a decent stretch near you. Follow the tips that I have given in this chapter and you won't go far wrong. The fish move a lot, and like their bait, be confident and you will enjoy some good sport. Keep your lines out of harms way and remain mobile. Remember to match your tackle to the situation and don't go in too light. Canals are littered with debris in places, so using light mono's when targeting big carp is not recommended. They are generally quite coloured so you don't need light lines, 10-12lb line is ideal coupled with strong hooklinks and hooks. I have really enjoyed today and it has re-ignited my fascination with them. Canals all over the country are stuffed with big carp! So dust the rods off, get out there and catch yourself a canal carp.

FLOATING AWAY

As the float slides under and another powerful carp tears off into the distance, I turn around and chuckle at the mickey takers who thought that float legering was a touch eccentric. Float fishing has become somewhat of a forgotten art in carp fishing, which is a shame. Nevertheless, for those of you that are willing to try it, the rewards are there. In this chapter were at the beautiful Bury Hill Fishery in Surrey to display exactly how to use and set up this method. The conditions are poor and with the air pressure through the roof and heavy overnight frosts, carp catching doesn't look too likely.

However, that isn't really the focus. The whole objective is to open your eyes to alternative carp fishing methods that don't cost a bomb, and more importantly, will put bonus fish on the bank in difficult conditions. Bury Hill is famed for its 'punts' that allow you to drift into nooks and crannies that can hold carp. It is also a place that I watched on the Go Fishing show, presented by John Wilson, where he was also afloat one of these punts, outwitting carp in the summer months during the early 1990s. The images of his float disappearing below the surface have never left me and to this day I still adore float fishing for carp.

I have often heard people say that float fishing is for 'jessies' but I can assure you that this method will produce carp on some of the most pressured venues in the country. It's not only exciting, it's also a very sensitive and accurate way of angling. This method isn't just for drifting around in a boat, it has many more strengths and is just as effective when used from the bankside. This method can give you major advantages over standard legering on numerous waters. Ironically, Bury Hill carp have been pressured with the float method for many years. However, how many of you can honestly say that you have seen people fishing with a float for carp on a regular basis on your water? I can't.

THE FLOAT LEDGER

Once again this set-up looks more complicated than it is, but actually it couldn't be simpler. Its nothing more than sliding a lock slide float onto your mainline before you add your lead system. Once again a method that is easy to use but underused.

01

The components that you will need are minimal.

02

Slide on your lock slide float.

03

When your line is slack the float will slide, when its tight it will lock.

04

Commence the tying of a simple leader knot by joining two lines and tying grinner knots. Here I am joining IQ to my Adrenaline mainline.

05

Tie a 5 turn grinner knot over each line with both the IQ and Adrenaline.

06

Wet the knot and pull tight slowly.

07

The finished knot should be small and compact.

08

Place a small amount of rig putty over the knot, both for protection and to help sink the line quicker.

09

I'm using a drop off in-line system at the other end due to the dense foliage and snags that I'm facing.

10

The rig is now finished and ready for tying the hooklink of your choice to.

One of the first things to fool the carp is the line angle. Most lakes will see lines of varying tensions extruding from the bankside, cutting through the depths until it reaches the lead. Carp are constantly coming into contact with the line and basically know they are being fished for, because they have come into contact with lines over a 10 to 100-yard area! With the float-legering method your line is basically holding in the surface layers and staying out the way of moving carp. This means that fish can move freely in your swim without coming into contact with lines at various points. The final interesting point is that fish often feel leadcore, tubing or Safe Zone leaders when they are feeding near the rig. With this method your line is coming down straight from the surface to within a couple of feet of your hook bait. This is a completely different angle from what they are used to, which means that fish will be far more comfortable than when they are feeding around conventional tactics. Day ticket carp have basically seen everything and I dare not think about how many times they must spook away from rigs or eject presentations.

This is the second key advantage with this approach. You are in the privileged position of being able to watch the float carefully and observe any sharp pulls or disappearing acts by the float, even if it means they do not materialise into full-blooded takes. At least you then know that you need to have a rethink on the rig front or have a recast! It's a very exciting style of fishing and also very sensitive because of the line angles. If fish do appear near to your rig you know about it because the float will 'bob' about. For once you know that your liners are caused by fish right by your rig, rather than at any point between the bank and your hook bait.

This is just the tip of the iceberg of information about the presentation, but I hope that you are beginning to build a picture of how you can gain an advantage on the man next door by adopting this tactic. If line angles and bite indication weren't enough for you, then have a think about this. Another element that I like, especially on silty lakes, is the way that it slows the lead down on its descent to the bottom of the lake. The Polaris float basically acts as a buoyancy aid and helps to slow it down. If you're fishing over silt or light weed this will act as a major advantage because it will give you a unique way of stopping the lead and bait from plugging into the soft stuff.

All you have to do is feed off some slack from the reel and let the float rise on a slack line to the surface. You then have a perfect marker float, which is sat directly above your hook bait. If you're clever, you can keep your hook bait in position and regularly feed on a little-and-often basis around the float, almost matchman style, to help induce some frenzied feeding. It's an exciting method seeing the float lift, twitch and shudder.

The construction of the rig couldn't be simpler; just follow the rig sequence. However, you can attach any type of rig that you want. Whether you want to use a lead clip, or running rig, you can use them all with this method. Simply slide the float onto your main line first and then set up your rig as you would do normally. The Polaris floats have a mechanism that basically locks the float in place when the line is tightened. Remember, float fishing shouldn't be a forgotten art, and it most certainly isn't sad. I still think that watching a float disappear below the surface is a million times more exciting than hearing my Delkims shriek into action. I get the same buzz now as I did when I was a little kid fishing for rudd.

It shouldn't be such an isolated method. The change of line angle, the sensitive bite indication, the visual aid, and all the other pros that this method brings, means that I'll be using it a lot more in my fishing. Hopefully some of you will give it a try in the near future, too.

THE FINAL FLOATIER

Layer Pits, in Colchester, where we find ourselves today, is a unique water. There are days when the fish are so active that you can see perhaps five fish a second jumping clean out of the water. It is an incredible sight and when you are on them you can have a frantic day. I've opted for a swim that gives me a view of the whole lake and I've already seen several fish crash on the wind line at around 60 yards. If they were to move to a different area I would notice immediately and could move swims accordingly.

The extra oxygen in the water has turned the fish on and it's as if they've had a dose of steroids. Every 10 seconds or so I notice huge, missile shaped commons erupt from the surface and belly flop back to the depths. I won't go into too much detail because I covered it in the last chapter, but the main advantage of float legering is offering the carp something different. When fish are pressured they will often become wary and a bite can be hard to come by. This method allows the line to lie on the surface and travel parallel below the float, rather than cutting through the water. I'm adamant that it can bring you more bites!

I'm soon steadying the float, preparing to cast towards an area of hard silt. I've been a member of Layer for several years and if there's one thing that I've learnt it's that the carp prefer to feed on the harder patches – not necessarily gravel, but the harder patches of silt that have been sifted for food. It could be that it contains more natural food, or that it's more appealing to feed on than the potent, choddier debris. I've been able to pinpoint this harder area by feeling the lead down using our Korda Probe lead.

Basically, I tie a lead to the end of the rod and feel it down to the lake bed. If it touches down with a soft resistance and plugs on the retrieve, I've hit an area of chod or a silty trough. Conversely, if it lands with a thud and draws back smoothly, I'm on the harder area. Once I've located the spot I pop the line in the clip, mark it with tape and tie on my float-ledgering rig.

I then punch my hook bait to the hard silt patch and feel the lead down to ensure that I've hit it accurately. I'm amazed at how far you can actually cast the float. It was a mere flick and the rig landed 60 yards out. When you talk to anglers about float fishing for carp they immediately think of margin fishing. However, in the right conditions I can cast to over 80 yards using this presentation, enabling me to cover most situations.

With my rig positioned on the spot I need to slowly pay out line from the spool. This allows the float to slide up the line towards the surface. The float is self-cocking so it will find the correct depth itself. That's the great thing about it – you can fish in deep water without the worry of a long tail that you'd struggle to cast.

As I peel off line I can feel the float rising to the surface due to the tight resistance on the line. It acts just like a marker float would when feature finding and gauging the depth. After paying off around seven feet of line the float pokes up and it's angling. I can now introduce a few free offerings. The other great advantage of using this method is that I have a permanent marker float out there to spod to. This once again ensures optimum accuracy – something that's paramount if you want to achieve consistent results.

I concoct a spod mix that includes items of hemp, corn and some new halibut pellets from Bait-Tech. This spruces the swim up and adds attraction around my dumbbell hook bait. Pressured carp have seen round boilies before and many raise their guard towards them. Thus, I like to use the Mainline Cell dumbbells – they provide a less obvious shape and complement my spod mix perfectly when tipped with a grain of imitation corn. One factor that's very important in my fishing is matching my hook bait to a particle in my spod mix. What's the point in gaining the carp's confidence on items in the spod mix if you're offering a completely different hook bait? It defeats the object of spodding. After 10 or so accurate spods we wait for the fish to move in and react to the bait.

FLOAT FISHING STICK MIX

To lure fish to my hookbait I'm using a really attractive stick mix that will be sure to stop carp in their tracks. You won't need many ingredients and it'll take only a few minutes to mix. You will realise once you've read this book just how highly I rate stick mixes of this ilk.

01
Add a couple of handfuls of 4mm Super Marine Halibut pellets from Bait-tech.

02
Now mix in a small tin of tuna in brine.

03
Add a small handful of sweetcorn to give the mix a little bit of colour.

04
Now add some of the mainline high impact fishy groundbait till it absorbs the juice from the tuna.

05
I'm using sticks to the size of the BOILIE Funnel web system, about an inch in length.

06
The finished mix is full of attraction ready to fool those wily carp.

It's clear that they like a bit of grub because they begin to crash literally yards from the tip of the float. All of a sudden the float cocks, lifts out of the water and then slides under the surface, leaving the clutch spinning. I'm onto it in a flash and soon battling it out with a Layer leviathan. The extra oxygen in the water gives the hooked fish a new lease of energy and it's putting up one heck of a tussle. Following steady pressure it's shaking its head in the deep margins, sending boils and bubbles upwards that cause creases on the surface. Before long a lovely, plated mirror carp is safely in the net and it looks to be all of 20lb. I recognise this fella. Layer is a water full of common carp and there's only a handful of mirrors, but they're very easy to identify due to the unique scale patterns. The last time I caught him he weighed 16lb, around five years ago. He looks a fair bit bigger now.

As I'm slipping the mirror back the other rod bursts into life. Action can come thick and fast when they get on the spod. Once again an epic fight ensues but this time it's a common – a real beauty, with dark, bronze flanks and huge, powerful rudders. The float is proving its worth, and while others are struggling behind bowstring-tight lines, another twenty slides into the net.

The carp seem to respond to the mix instantly, so I decide to top up the swim with a further six spods. I follow this with the two hook baits and it doesn't take long for another one to ramp off. Unfortunately, disaster strikes and it manages to shake its head just before netting, causing the hook to pop out. It's thoroughly enjoyable watching a float rather than sitting static behind bite alarms.

The action is non-stop with another 10 or so carp taken to this method - an awesome day on the float ledger method. Give it a try, it's great fun!

WINTER STALKING

It surprises me just how many people stay indoors when the cold weather arrives. However it's not the eighties anymore, and winters seem to be a lot milder these days. I think for many of you starting fishing or being the occasional visitor to the bank, it's important to realise just how prolific winter sport can be.

On today's session I have decided to visit a small mature pool in deepest darkest Essex! This is unlike commercial carp pools. The fish here are small, however they are 'old 'and stunted which gives them a unique character which has kept me revisiting this little intimate place ever since I first wet a line there back in the early nineties as a 'wee nipper'. I used to love this lake when I first started carping and I have been coming here ever since. Even though my fishing now is focused around catching 30lb+ carp,

I have never been one to fish just for big fish. I love the buzz of catching fish and these old creatures have real character to them. So what if they're not massive, any of you out there, should always judge a capture on its merits, not just how big a fish is. I felt this lake reflected a scenario that many of you will face on a local club lake, a small lake with a good head of carp that can tend to do a disappearing act when the cold sets in. The fishing here in the summer can be unbelievable with a wonderful evenings fishing possible on a small ledger outfit, pellets and a few boilie hookbaits. However today will be much harder due to seasonal conditions, the key to winter success is finding them!

I posed myself with a scenario to prove to you all, that instead of spending a sunday lunchtime at home on the couch catching nothing, that one rod, a net and a bit of bait can give you a wonderful afternoons sport. I am literally visiting this lake for a couple of hours, armed with my 6ft Tribal travel rod and net, a small bag of pellets, some bread crumb and an assortment of hookbaits. The day chair, and heavy gear was left at home. My plan was to try and find fish right under the bank and try to catch them at close quarters.

This lake has lots of little corners and has a Dam wall at one end which you would normally head straight to in the winter due to the deeper water. However the little 'monkeys' had decided the most comfortable place was not the deep water off the dam, but the silty shallow water under the tree lined area of the lake. This was to be my first port of call today.

As I gently crept up to the bank with my polarized glasses on, I could just make out the shape of a 'static' carp in the gin clear water. I signalled to Gareth the photograper to make his way over and take some pictures. There soon appeared to be a couple of fish in the area. I can't stress enough just how critical location is in the winter. Gareth made an interesting point whilst we were chatting, he explained that some of the biggest carp bags in the matches come in the winter.

The reason for this is simple, the fish tend to end up in a 'ball' which means if you can find them, you will have some excellent results. Well it appeared that I had found where the fish were, so Gareth set me a target of catching one within an hour and a half. My first plan was to feed a couple of spots with a bit of my bread crumb and pellet combo. This would get the fish having a little grub around and will hopefully help to colour the water up, because as it stood I was very wary about putting a hookbait in without getting the fish feeding first such was the clarity of the water. I baited 3 spots with a handful of bait on each spot, just enough to interest a couple of fish to feed within inches of the bank. I then nestled away in the undergrowth to rig up my rod. I was just going to fish a little float ledger set-up that I really like. It is based around a sliding float set-up and adds a more exciting element to standard ledgering. Coupled with a 6ft rod and 6lb reel line, the sport should I hook one, would be awesome.

Once the rod was set up, I took a stroll through the undergrowth to peer through the trees and investigate some of the spots. 2 out of the 3 spots appeared to have fish feeding on them because the water had clouded up and the odd 'oily' tale pattern was breaking the surface. Who said winter fishing was boring? My heart started racing at the thought of fooling one of these old wily carp into making a mistake. I had my first rod at the ready, a small size 12 Wide Gape hook was attached knotless knot style to a 10lb 1Q2 fluorocarbon hooklink. I had decided to use a little PVA stick of bread crumb, pellets and corn. My hookbait might seem bizarre, but it was a piece of fake bread that was cut down so it would just sink to the bottom with the weight of the hook.

I was using a light hookbait to combat the silty conditions. I was standing as still as a mannequin with the rod in my hand remembering a scene at Redmire pool with Chris Yates during the amazing Passion for Angling fishing series where he stuck a scarecrow into the shallow water to familiarise the fish with his existence, so that when he finally angled for them, the fish where not overly concerned with a human shadow impeding on their watery home. I was stood with the rod in hand waiting for the fish on the spot to turn round so that I could lower the rig down and wait for them to turn their attentions back to this little spot.

The two fish that I could see gently backed off and gave me a moment's peace and allowed me to lower my rig. I watched the PVA bag melt just in time for the fish to return. Most of the fish in this lake are around the 5-7lb mark but these two seemed a bit bigger and I could see why as they gently fed around my hookbait avoiding it like it had a hook attached to it. It got to the stage when the fish were directly over my hookbait only for them to move off and my hookbait remained in exactly the same spot.

THE WINTER FLOAT RIG

Just like actually getting out there and doing a spot of winter stalking, the method itself is very exciting. This little float rig is nothing extravagant but on a cold winters day it gives me something to look at rather than staring at a bite alarm or bobbin. The float helps to show line bites and obviously sail away bites!

01 Take a small self cocking waggler.

02 Remove the plug-in self cocking weight.

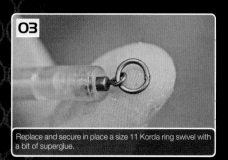
03 Replace and secure in place a size 11 Korda ring swivel with a bit of superglue.

04 Now thread your mainline through the ring swivel.

05 Take a small 1.5oz Flatliner pear and Shockleader sleeve (trimmed down).

06 Slide on your lead tapered end first, followed by the shockleader sleeve thin end first.

07
Now tie on a ring swivel.

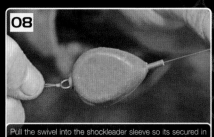
08
Pull the swivel into the shockleader sleeve so its secured in place and semi-fixed.

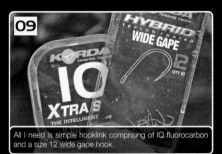
09
All I need is simple hooklink comprising of IQ fluorocarbon and a size 12 wide gape hook.

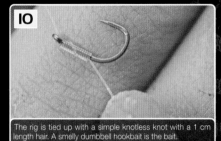
10
The rig is tied up with a simple knotless knot with a 1 cm length hair. A smelly dumbbell hookbait is the bait.

11
Take pinch of mixed micro pellets.

12
Tie off a small 50p sized Funnel web bag.

30mins gone and the carp were winning already, but both Gareth and I where buzzing at the excitement. The fish had moved off and I was certain that they had a problem. I moved the 5 or so metres around the corner to look at the other spot I had baited which was receiving some attention. I gently poked my head between a gap in quite a big tree and low and behold there they where, noses in the mud feeding on my little handful of bait. I decided to trickle in a few mini combo pellets on top just to keep the fish enthused and to increase their feeding intensity. My next job was to attach a hookbait that they where likely to snap up. I hair rigged two bits of corn on the hair, surely this would have em'? I got the rig in without disturbing the carp which where literally no more than 1ft from the bank in probably 18inches of water. The number of fish had increased to 6-8 fish and my hookbait was right under them. The float was continuously moving and bobbing as the fish were catching it with their tales. The carp here seemed so much bigger than the average stamp, more around the 12-14lb mark than the single figures that I expected. Surely it was only a matter of time. I just could not get my hookbait picked up, and then a carp got too carried away and managed to give me a huge line bite and they did the off! 2-nil to the carp!

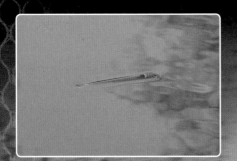

Bites on the float are so exciting with this rig.
You normally get a lift before it sails away.

I decided to let the swim breathe for 10mins or so and introduced some more pellet and within minutes they were back! This time I decided to attach a dumbell shaped boilie by Mainline baits. My float ledger set-up was once again back in amongst the fish in the shallow water. The bigger fish were feeding. I was trickling in single 5mm pellets every few seconds to keep the fish on the spot, and within about 2mins a small common shot into the swim,

Gareth and I could not believe that a bite had not been forthcoming such was the preoccupation of the fish and then out the blue; 'BANG' I saw the fish dart off and the little common shaking its head on the bottom then darting off along with my rig attached to it! Fish on. After a good scrap a beautiful winter carp was in the folds of the net. Phew, 1 hour and 20mins into the session and the mission was accomplished.

I managed one more bite before the session was out, but the fish came off due to a hook pull. It was now time to take Gareth for a trotting session on the River Stour in search of chub and roach! However the whole focus of the session was to prove how enjoyable winter fishing can be. If you're not up for a long day session, then choose your venue carefully, and spend a couple of hours down there and you'll be surprised at just how much fun the fishing will be.

Bait a few spots and use your eyes to locate the fish. Once you find the fish in the winter, the hard part is done because catching them really isn't rocket science.

THEORY WORKS

For the final piece in this section I've taken a day away to visit a venue for the first time in absolutely bitter sub zero temperatures in late January. The lake is on the coast in Mersea, Essex. A small club water with a decent stock of doubles, but in these conditions it will be very difficult to locate and catch carp in these temperatures and poor easterly wind.

The idea is to put into practice some of the key principles and theories that I have been harping on about throughout this book. They are not 'bullet-proof' elements, but I believe, if you follow my list of priorities in your fishing, you will be heading in the right direction to success very quickly.

WATERCRAFT

You can have all the gizmo's, bait and super rigs, but if your watercraft doesn't take priority you will fail miserably, or at the very best be made to look an idiot by other anglers who haven't got all the kit, but are at least presenting their less superior rigs and tackle in front of fish. Today I have taken time to walk around the lake and look for areas that scream carp. The obvious place is the large reed beds on the opposite bank to where I've parked my van. However with this easterly wind it's important to find reed beds that are in the lee of the wind and not facing into this awfully cold wind. Refer back to that first chapter in the book and note how I discourage anglers from fishing in the teeth of an easterly wind during cold snaps. It's as uninviting to the fish, as it is to us. Having surveyed the area for a good half hour, I have seen no fish movement, but I've noticed a couple of sheltered areas on the far bank reeds that through experience scream carp. This area looks more comfortable and somewhere that I expect the carp to be laying up in during this cold weather.

Do all you can to enhance your watercraft, but bear in mind that whilst it's the single most important element of fishing, its also the hardest to learn. To some, it comes naturally, whilst to others, only hours on the bank can help them develop this timeless skill.

PIN-POINT ACCURACY

Having now parked myself in the furthest swim from the car park, I set about getting my rigs in place. Tactics for today would be single bright visual pop-ups, finished off with a 50p sized funnel web bag of pellets, groundbait and tuna. On any new water where I expect the fish to be laying up due to the cold, I'll always make a start with this approach. In fact on this trip I've come armed with nothing but my tub of hookbaits and PVA bag mixture. That is how strongly I'm putting the onus of my session on fish location and casting accuracy. Master these elements and you're three quarters of the way there.

I have a large reed bed to my left about 60 yards down my margin, however this is facing straight into the bitter wind. However on my far margin is another large expanse of reeds, but this time, these are more sheltered with a decent sized area of calm water protruding from them. If the carp are anywhere, they'll be here.

Simple, bright and smelly, it front of fish it will produce bites.

TIE THE MULTI RIG

This rig has burst onto the carp scene in the last few years mainly down to the fishing of an angler called Jon Macallister. He's caught from some of hardest venues in the country on this set-up. However the rig was first invented by Mike Kavanagh. This rig is simple to tie but also very adaptable and great when you need to change hooks.

01

You will need some Choddy hooks, rig rings and a coated braid.

02

Firstly tie a figure of eight loop around an inch in length at one end of your coated hooklink. Make sure you do this with the coating still on the material.

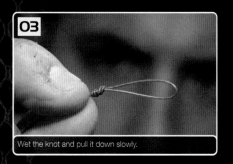

03

Wet the knot and pull it down slowly.

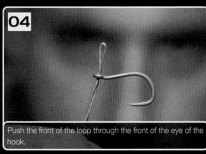

04

Push the front of the loop through the front of the eye of the hook.

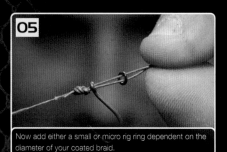

05

Now add either a small or micro rig ring dependent on the diameter of your coated braid.

06

Fold the loop of the knot back over the hook.

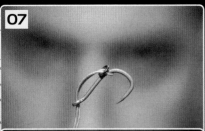

07

Pull the loop down till your rig ring is positioned like so.

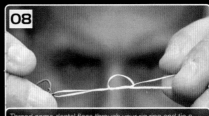

08

Thread some dental floss through your rig ring and tie a two turn slip knot into it. This will help secure your hookbait in place.

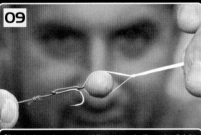

09

Slide the knot down around the pop-up boilie and pull tight.

10

Blob the end of the knot with a lighter, be careful not to burn through the knot!

Now simply reveal a small amount of the hooklinks inner core then add a split shot so the rig sinks nice and slowly! Your multi-rig is now ready for multiple captures!

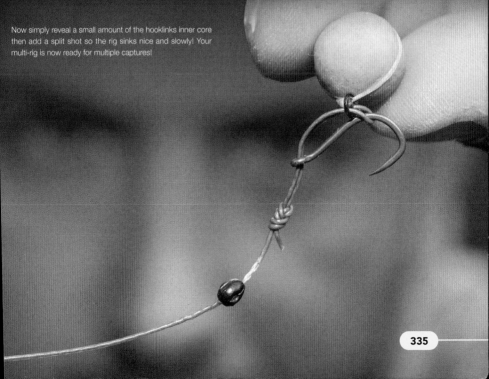

Again I covered how important feeling the lead down and clipping up is in my fishing. It is another element that will turn you from Mr average to Mr excellent! I had a few casts to edge myself close to the reeds and then put the line under the line clip. Whilst edging up to the reeds I always stop the cast prior to hitting water and ensure my rod tip is pointing up to the air. Again in the 'clipping up ' chapter, I explained how by keeping the rod tip high and line tight, you can feel the lead touch down onto the lakebed. This helps to tell me exactly what type of bottom I'm fishing, which in turn dictates the type of rig and presentation that I will use. Additionally through experience, you will be able to assess the approximate depth that you are fishing in. I normally say that I second equals about 3ft in water depth, so when the lead hits the water on a tight line, and you start counting, you should be able to get a rough idea of depth.

Such was my confidence in the far bank reed bed, I decided to place two rods over to that spot. Both areas felt firm with a depth of around 6ft. I was confident my smelly bright pop-up and bag would do the damage. The other rod, was going to act as a roving rod, which I would use to try and scope out fish from the open water area. However I thoroughly expect the reed rods to produce the goods.

One thing that has become obvious over years of winter fishing, is just how good lunch time is for a bite. High noon and a bright winter sun just seems to activate the fish enough to raise them from their semi dormant state and inject some feeding life into them. This session was no different. My rods had been out a couple of hours on this horrendously cold session when the left hand rod, fished tight to the reeds was away. The carp were exactly where I thought they were, hiding in the lee of the wind! After a spirited winter battle, a beautiful chestnut coloured mirror rolled over the draw cord and into the waiting net! Job done.

THE TOP 3 COMMANDMENTS

The rest of the session past without event, with nothing else being caught by any other anglers, this just proved how important watercraft is. It ensured that, during the short feeding spell when the carp switched on to feed, I had a rig EXACTLY where they were.

If you were to take THREE elements from this whole series of chapters, it would be:
● Watercraft/Fish location   ● Accurate casting   ● Efficient rigs/bait

Follow these in that order and you will notice your fishing and results improve with every session.

ACKNOWLEDGMENTS

Well there we have it, my first book is complete and hopefully not the last.
With methods evolving, developing and new innovations arriving all the time,
I'm sure it won't be long before I have a new pool of idea's to present to a new
wave of anglers in the future.

I've really enjoyed seeing this book come together and I've got to thank the
guys at MPRESS especially Paul Moulder who has put up with all my nagging
and demands during the design and layout of the book. Hopefully the style was
a refreshing change from what you've seen or read elsewhere.

Once again a special thank you to Marc Coulson, Kevin Wilmot and David Hall
Publishing for collating the hundreds of photo's that you've seen in this book.
These have been taken throughout years of working with their titles, and was
critical in the production of this book. I must also mention friend Gareth Purnell
who worked with me on so many of these chapters. He shared many of the on
bank, experiences whilst working at DHP and took so many of the pictures in
this book.

If you've read this far, thank you. I hope you take some of the tips and tactics
in this book and utilise them on your future fishing trips. Nothing in this book
is gimmicky or pointless, I've covered it, because it catches fish.

Get out there catch some fish, but most of all enjoy and savour your time on
the bank because after all that's the unique element that bonds us all, the
whole, and unique carp fishing experience.

It's time for a beer, until next time, here's a toast
to your next success.

Ali Hamidi